MENTAL
AND
EMOTIONAL
RELEASE®

DR. MATT JAMES WITH TRIS THORP

BALBOA.
PRESS
A DIVISION OF HAY HOUSE

Balboa Press books may be ordered through booksellers or by contacting:

Balboa Press
A Division of Hay House
1663 Liberty Drive
Bloomington, IN 47403
www.balboapress.com
1 (877) 407-4847

Because of the dynamic nature of the Internet, any web addresses or
links contained in this book may have changed since publication and
may no longer be valid. The views expressed in this work are solely those
of the author and do not necessarily reflect the views of the publisher,
and the publisher hereby disclaims any responsibility for them.

The author of this book does not dispense medical advice or prescribe
the use of any technique as a form of treatment for physical, emotional,
or medical problems without the advice of a physician, either directly
or indirectly. The intent of the author is only to offer information
of a general nature to help you in your quest for emotional and
spiritual well-being. In the event you use any of the information in
this book for yourself, which is your constitutional right, the author
and the publisher assume no responsibility for your actions.

The information, ideas, and suggestions in this book are not
intended as a substitute for professional advice. Before following
any suggestions contained in this book, you should consult your
personal physician or mental health professional. Neither the
author nor the publisher shall be liable or responsible for any
loss or damage allegedly arising as a consequence of your use or
application of any information or suggestions in this book.

Any people depicted in stock imagery provided by Thinkstock are
models, and such images are being used for illustrative purposes only.
Certain stock imagery © Thinkstock.

Print information available on the last page.

ISBN: 978-1-5043-8450-6 (sc)
ISBN: 978-1-5043-8451-3 (e)

Library of Congress Control Number: 2017911418

Balboa Press rev. date: 09/26/2017

Contents

Foreword

"Who am I meant to be? Will I ever find the person that I'm meant to be with? How can I truly be happy? What is my true purpose in life?"

These are pretty big questions, and they're questions that have plagued me since I was a small child.

After sneaking into my parents' bedroom at the age of five and seeing my father meditating, I decided that was something I wanted to do. My mom taught me how to meditate, gave me a mantra, and sent me on my merry way. Meditation really helped me rein in my consciousness and my energy. It helped me to relax my young mind and find a calm state. I was still very young when I heard a swami from India talk about consciousness. Though I was barely in grammar school at the time, I remember him saying that our entire reality is in our mind.

Really? That didn't seem possible. How can everything that I experience be right here in my head? Furthermore, if that's true, it means I have control over my happiness. It means I have the ability to make my life the way that I want it. It means that I'm responsible for my experiences. That was a lot of heavy-duty thinking for an eight-year-old to process.

A life-changing moment came for me at the age of twelve when I got to do a fire walk with Anthony Robbins. I'd heard others say things like, "Everything is in your mind," and "You have the ability to become empowered as an individual if you can change your mind," long before I heard Tony say it. In fact, from the time that I was a little kid, I'd heard a bunch of different people say, "If you're free of your fear, if you're free from your negative emotions, if you're free to control your mind, you can begin creating a world anyway you want."

But the difference *that* day was that we went outside and walked on twelve feet of burning hot coals to prove it.

I didn't have to be a genius to know that fire burns. Yet after walking across those red hot coals, my feet seemed pretty okay. Needless to say, as a twelve-year-old, that experience shook my world up a bit. Suddenly I had evidence, proof, an undeniable experience that my thoughts could affect my outcomes.

Whoa …

I attended a few more fire walks before I went on to take a practitioner training in Neuro Linguistic Programming (NLP) at the age of thirteen. This training was another defining moment in my life, for it taught me the power of language and deepened my understanding of the mind-body connection. I became a Master Practitioner of NLP before I entered high school. In the NLP Master Practitioner training, I witnessed individuals release phobias and other deep-seated negative patterns, serious patterns and issues that most professionals claimed could not be released that easily.

But they were.

After high school, I began to work for my father's company, and I began to teach this "self-empowerment" stuff. I decided I wanted to look at human empowerment from a more academic perspective as well, so I went back to school and became a Doctor of Integrative Health Psychology. (That's a fancy way of saying I studied the mind-body-energy connection.)

This path brought me to where I am today. It's helped me to understand not just a mind-body connection, but the inherent potential for empowerment each of us has inside.

In the late 1990s and early 2000s, I was able to work

with Dr. Bruce Lipton, who wrote *The Biology of Belief.* When his book came out in 2005, it was a defining moment for me as a teacher. His book starts off by saying that any *scientist* reading the book will basically say, "Yeah, we already know this stuff." He goes on to say something that I'd would like to echo: What we've been taught through the media, through Hollywood, through common cultural philosophy is that we are at the whim of certain elements and unable to change them.

But as scientists will affirm, that's simply not true.

Over the past few decades, I've taught dozens of groups and thousands of students every year. These days, I start off by saying this is my favorite time to teach. Not only is there scientific *evidence* of the mind-body connection, it's been around for three decades at least. Not only is there evidence of the existence of energy but scientific researchers have validated that energy affects our cells—*and* our reality, first and foremost. Not only is there evidence that you can have freedom from your fear, but those symptoms, diseases, and issues the media claims you have no control over? We now have evidence that you *do* have control. You can release seemingly immovable, impenetrable issues and be free of them forever.

This book is focused on the technique I teach called Mental and Emotional Release (MER) therapy. I get to spend my life teaching people that the baggage they have been told is *real* is no more real than that bad dream you had a few nights ago. Imagine for a moment if you could be free from your baggage, free from your limitations, and free from the pain. How different would your life be?

What we all want is happiness. But you can't be happy when you're filled with anger, sadness, fear, hurt, or guilt. You can't find those amazing connections if you have limiting beliefs about yourself. And you can't find your purpose, that person you're meant to be in this life, those things you're meant to do, and those things that you're meant to have *unless* you clear out the garbage that's blocking you. In fact, with that garbage still in the way, you won't even be able to *see* possibilities for yourself, much less *live* them.

I'm not here to tell you that this book is going to transform your life. I'm here to give you hope. If you walk away from this book simply knowing that you *can* be free from your limitations, then I've done my job. I know of so many techniques that can help people become who and what they desire to be. I happen to like this particular one — MER — because of my personal experience with it and what I've seen it do for so many people in all of the years I've taught it.

My students know that I love to tell stories and engage in conversation. I've done my best to make this book a conversation. For those of you who like statistics with the validation and the research, feel free to skip ahead. The studies outlined in chapter 12 will give you what your left brain needs to know this stuff is real. Or you can just begin at the beginning, as I describe this technique and the amazing results my students and I have seen from it.

I want to give credit to so many individuals for helping this book come together. First, my thanks to Tris Thorp, who wrote chapter 4, about emotions and emotional baggage. Four others who made significant contributions are Dr. Larry Momaya, Dr. Patrick Scott, Dr. Tracey Coley, and Dr. Rose Johnson. These four are not only students of mine, they are colleagues who have helped me to validate this work that I've been doing for three decades. They, along with several of my students, have shared their personal and client stories to help illustrate MER and its potential. This book would not be possible if not for all of them.

Mahalo.

Dr. Matt

Introduction

We'll call him David.[1]

David was a patient of one of my students, Dr. Larry Momaya, a board-certified psychiatrist and brain-imaging expert in Southern California who was motivated to find alternatives to the psychotropic medications he commonly prescribed. Dr. Momaya had studied with me to become a Master Practitioner in 2010. Here is David's story, as Dr. Momaya told it to me:

> David was referred to me by his therapist when he was about seventeen or eighteen. When David came to me, he had been diagnosed with depression, anxiety, and ADD, and he had some history of drug abuse. While the therapist continued seeing David for therapy, I worked with him on a course of antidepressants and antianxiety meds. David did okay but was never fully symptom free.
>
> After I'd seen David for about three and a half years, he started complaining of severe abdominal pain. The pain continued and worsened, and over the next year, he

---

[1]   The case studies and examples in this book are real, but we have intentionally changed names and details throughout to protect clients' privacy.

was referred to a series of specialists, who couldn't figure out what the heck was going on. But they started David on various pain meds: morphine, barbiturates, and finally a fentanyl patch. Nothing really worked. David still suffered, and I could see that the combination of all those meds was taking its toll on him. I reviewed all the medications he was taking and realized that a) they weren't really resolving the physical pain or the emotional issues and b) he was maxed out on the dosages he was taking and running out of options.

So one day I asked David, "Are you open to trying something different for your pain?"

He basically said, "What have I got to lose?"

I ran him through a simple hypnosis technique that reduced his pain from a 10 to a 2. That was really encouraging—for both of us —but I knew we needed to tackle David's problems at the source or they would surface in other ways.

I introduced him to the concept of the Mental and Emotional Release (MER) therapy. David was initially hesitant, but we worked with the process slowly. At each session, he would release more of the negative emotions that had controlled his life up to that point. As we progressed, he was able to reduce his meds, first the antianxiety and antidepressants, then finally the pain medications. Within three months, he was off everything completely and experiencing no physical pain, no anxiety, and no depression.

I attended David's wedding about a year later. He was fully functioning, very happy, and totally free of any medication. This is the type of result we all want for all of our patients. But frankly, before I started introducing MER to my patients, I rarely saw it and definitely didn't see it happening as quickly as this.

Like Dr. Momaya, I've witnessed amazing shifts and outcomes myself, using MER, with a few Davids. I've worked with and taught the Mental and Emotional Release technique for years now, and I've seen it achieve extraordinary results in all kinds of mental and emotional disorders ranging from depression, post-traumatic stress disorder (PTSD), and extreme phobias to simple behavioral issues like procrastination and poor social skills. I've also heard dozens of success stories from other therapists and Master Practitioners I've trained in the MER process. The stories range from clients overcoming alcohol and drug addiction or debilitating anxiety to those breaking through barriers to achieve career success or happiness in their relationships.

And these results happen within *hours*, not years or months.

As I previously explained, my motivation for writing this book is pretty simple. My mission in life and the mission of my company, the Empowerment Partnership, is to empower the planet. Or more specifically, to help people empower themselves, which will in turn, empower the planet. And I can't think of a better way to help empower the planet than by spreading information that can help heal and empower us all as individuals, can you?

In my experience and in the experience of the many psychotherapists and Master Practitioners who use it, MER is effective, with little to no relapse after treatment is concluded. It's also extremely efficient and often gets positive results within the first session—even with problems like David's that were long lasting or had not responded to other treatments. And that's empowering.

I've written this book to spread the word about the Mental and Emotional Release technique and to give you hope that it is possible to overcome the baggage you carry. Within these pages, you'll get an overview of MER, a basic understanding of the process, and how and why it works as well as it does. You'll read a number of case studies of real-life clients who have sought help with a variety of issues, and you'll see the results they achieved through the process. And at the end of the book, I'll share some of the recent research on MER.

I've written this book in language that's accessible to nontherapists, and it's my intention to give you a good understanding of the Mental and Emotional Release technique in these pages. I hope the case studies inspire you to investigate MER and Neuro Linguistic Programming (NLP) further. Whether you are suffering from a debilitating illness such as depression or looking to enhance your experience of life and performance by releasing negative emotions of anger, fear, sadness, hurt, and guilt, MER may well be the key you're looking for.

But this book will *not* give you the foundation necessary to really use MER effectively unless you've had training in NLP. And I definitely do not recommend that you attempt to use this technique on yourself or others who have severe disorders such as PTSD or depression *unless* you're a qualified psychotherapist with extensive training in NLP and MER. If MER sounds like a good option for you, please contact our office at (800) 800-MIND or DrMatt.com to learn about our trainings or find a qualified Master Practitioner to guide you through the MER process.

If you're a therapist who would like to see more positive results in your work with clients, I encourage you to read the material and review the research in chapter 12. If you think this might be a good complement to your practice, you'll find information on professional training and certification in MER on our website, EmpowermentPartnership.com, or my personal site at DrMatt.com.

Getting this technique out to the psychotherapeutic community right now is critical. In 2011, the Substance Abuse and Mental Health Services Administration issued the results of their five-year study on mental health in the United States. It found that over forty-five million Americans—approximately one in five adults—suffer from some form of mental illness. According to the CDC, diagnoses of mental illness in children have also risen sharply. That increase might be due in part to changes in diagnostic measures. But the CDC also reports that "suicide is the third leading cause of death in young people between ten and twenty-four, many of whom had mental and emotional disorders."[2]

We're in a mental and emotional health crisis, and we spend an estimated $147.4 billion on mental health care annually in the United States.[3] Yet, according to Glenn Waller, chairman of the psychology department at the University of Sheffield and one of the authors of the 2009 meta-analysis conducted by leading mental health professionals in the United Kingdom and the United States, "A large number of people with mental health problems that could be straightforwardly addressed are getting therapies that have *very little chance of being effective*."[4]

To me, that is sad—and preventable.

When I was studying to become a Doctor of Psychology, the professor in my health psychology class talked about certain villages in China that approach mental emotional

---

[2] http://www.cdc.gov/violenceprevention/pub/youth_suicide.html

[3] http://alumni.stanford.edu/get/page/magazine/article/?article_id=64350

[4] *New York Times* article by Harriet Brown dated March 25, 2013.

and physical health in a very different way than the typical Western approach. In some of these villages, the doctors are paid every month by the entire village when everyone is healthy. When someone becomes ill, that family is no longer required to pay. The professor looked out us and said, "Imagine a health care system where professionals are paid to keep people *healthy* rather than making money off of illness."

I grew up in a family that emphasized reframing an issue or looking at things from a different perspective. So I loved the professor's example of such a different perspective than ours, and it got me thinking. Our system pays people to treat and prevent illness. A fundamental cornerstone of health or integrative psychology is *wellness promotion* as opposed to *illness prevention*. Those who work in wellness promotion understand that mental and emotional health and well-being are an integral part of that wellness. This is why I believe the technique of MER is so vital: It supports wellness on all levels.

A Brief History of MER

I built the Mental and Emotional Release process on a specific technique, Time Line Therapy, that my father, Dr. Tad James, developed in 1985. He, in turn, based his Time Line Therapy on the neurolinguistic programming theories and practices of Richard Bandler and John Grinder, the founders of NLP.

Why is MER based on NLP?

A few years ago, I went back to school to get my PhD in Integrative Health Psychology. At that time, I'd been working with NLP for about twenty-five years and wanted to see if there was another approach to therapy and personal growth that was even better than NLP.

Honestly, I didn't find anything better.

I studied allopathic, complementary, and traditional psychological therapies. But nothing was as effective and efficient in dealing with the broad spectrum of mental and emotional health issues as NLP. So though I've incorporated some information from other therapeutic practices into the NLP trainings I do, I still focus on NLP because it gets results—not just for me, but for the hundreds of therapists I've trained.

The Time Line Therapy technique my father created was so effective that the Council of Psychotherapy in Croatia asked him to train them in it to help deal with the thousands of Croatian victims of the war, who were suffering from post-traumatic stress disorder. At that time, PTSD—which is ranked as the most extreme of negative emotions, like a phobia on steroids—had hit epidemic proportions in Croatia. The council had tested several therapies to respond to the crisis. But they found that Time Line Therapy was the only one that worked 100 percent of the time with no relapses.

I began working with Time Line Therapy in 1993. Since that time, I've modified the technique to some extent based on feedback from my clients, students, and practitioners to obtain even more impressive results. I now teach this refined technique as the Mental and Emotional Release process to hundreds of students every year in our Master Practitioner courses. The body of incredible results continues to expand.

Comparing MER to Other Therapies

Compared to other types of therapy, Mental and Emotional Release therapy has a number of benefits. First of all, MER is fast. Rather than spending months or years in therapy, most problems and symptoms—even those caused by severe trauma or those that have been ingrained for decades—will literally disappear within one or two sessions, a total of five to eight hours. In fact, one of the odd downsides of the process is that it works so quickly and thoroughly to eradicate long-standing issues that clients have a hard time believing it. They feel symptom free yet may have trouble trusting such a dramatic shift that happened with so swiftly and easily.

Several years ago, I demonstrated part of the MER process in one of my workshops. I asked for a volunteer, and a woman we'll call Mona responded. Mona had seen a variety of psychologists for ten years because of her anger issues. Her volatile and almost constant anger had cost her a marriage as well as several jobs, and she was beginning to see that it was affecting her health. But the therapies she tried over the years didn't get rid of this anger, and she had given up completely.

I gave Mona a brief explanation of MER, where we unearth and revisit the root cause of her anger. She agreed to let me guide her through the technique. Ten minutes later, she opened her eyes, with happy tears streaming down her face. She looked at me and said, "My anger has disappeared. Why did I waste all that time in therapy?" That statement was quickly followed by, "Wait, that was too easy. How do I know if it is really gone?"

The discussion I had with Mona after the release took longer than the release itself. I had to explain why it is possible to let negative emotions go, and added that we do it all the time. Three years later, I saw Mona again, and she immediately said, "I am not sure why it was so easy, but it worked."

The positive changes that happen during MER often feel so integrated and natural, clients even have trouble remembering that they ever felt differently. The new shift feels so authentic that it simply feels like who they are, as in the following example:

A student of mine worked with a three-pack-a-day smoker who wanted to quit. George had been a chain smoker for decades but his doctor—and George's wife—finally gave him the ultimatum that he had to quit. For years, George had tried nicotine patches and gum, herbs, even acupuncture. Nothing worked for longer than a day. As he put it, "Cigarettes have me by the throat. There's nothing I can do to stop."

My student took George through some NLP techniques and some hypnosis in one three-hour session. Two weeks later, George returned, complaining that the process hadn't worked. "I'm still smoking," he said.

Surprised, my student asked, "How much?"

"Three cigarettes a day."

My student guided George through a few more processes and arranged for a follow-up call the next week.

That next week, George reported that he had stopped smoking completely. "But it wasn't that MER stuff you did with me," he claimed. "I just decided I wanted to quit. No big deal."

As my student told me, "George didn't even remember that cigarettes had him 'by the throat' a few weeks before that."

Why does it work so quickly?

I'm often asked in class why MER works so easily and quickly. The answer is actually really simple. Think of the last time you got over something. In my trainings, I always ask, "How many of you have ever been afraid of something that you're no longer afraid of? Or alternatively, how many of you have been angry at something that you're no longer angry at?" Without fail, most (if not all) of my students raise their hands.

Next, I'll say, "Great. And how long did it take to get over your anger or fear?" In the twenty-plus years I've done this, the answer from the group always ranges from "immediately" to "twenty years." In a recent training in San Diego, a lady clearly stated that it took her over twenty years to get over the anger related to her ex-husband.

I said, "Great; let's go with this one."

I asked this woman to be a little bit more specific. "From the moment you went from being angry with him to no longer being angry with him, how long did that take?"

9

She said (as most everyone does), "That was instantaneous."

I then asked, "Wouldn't be fair to say that it took twenty years for you to be *ready* to let go of the anger? But the moment you were ready to let it go, it happened in an instant?"

And just like everyone else in my experience, she admitted that yes, that was true.

When I was in school, I asked my professor about this. My cognitive psychology textbook said that you can go from having a great day to a completely bad day in an instant. A phobia can be created in an instant. The textbook went on to say that will take decades to overcome a phobia.

So I asked the professor, "Why is it that the neurology of an individual can go from good to bad in an instant, but not from bad to good in an instant?"

His answer was quite interesting. He said many therapists and academic psychologists have lost the focus on the client and now focus on the research instead. He didn't paint this as either good or bad, just a statement of the current affairs in psychology.

He went on to say that he believed I should continue to teach what I teach because it's built on the premise that people go from bad to good instantaneously.

The caveat is, are you ready to let bad go?

No Need to Dig up Old Bodies

Another benefit of MER is that it's not necessary to delve into old content. (As we'll discuss in the next chapter, a practitioner looks for *context*, not content.) Clients don't have to retell the stories of their old painful wounds or embarrassments. They aren't asked to describe how they were potty trained or every past relationship they ever had. They don't even describe their symptoms in very much detail.

For example, Mona never had to give me any detailed

information about her anger or its history in her life. She didn't have to describe her childhood or the details of any of her ruined relationships or past business failures. In fact, it was only *after* the release that Mona explained that much of her anger was focused towards her mother. (By the end of our two-week workshop, Mona shared with the group how good her relationship with her mother had become and how wonderful she now thought her mom was.)

The interesting thing is that some people actually have an issue with this. We have been so trained through talk shows and reality TV that drama is somehow a part of life. As a result, we expect change to be dramatic. Fortunately, change does *not* need to be dramatic (which I'll admit isn't very good for TV ratings). Some people have trouble letting go of the idea that change is difficult.

I remember one student who volunteered to help me demonstrate MER.

His issue simply disappeared, and he said, "That was too easy. I should have at least cried."

All I could say was, "Hey, I'm sorry that it was so easy and so drama-free."

No Need to Relive the Trauma

One of the most valuable benefits of MER is that the process does *not* require clients to re-experience the events that traumatized them in the first place. This is especially important for clients with PTSD or phobias or those suffering from chronic depression or anxiety that is tied to abuse or trauma of some sort. The downside of many other therapies is that they require clients to "re-traumatize" themselves and relive the experience: a distressful process that many clients simply can't face.

But during MER, clients are able to remain disassociated from disturbing events of the past. If they do observe painful memories, MER techniques keep clients at a safe distance, helping them adopt a perspective that feels empowered and safe.

One of my students worked with a client, Marcie, who had come from a severely abusive home. Marcie had been terrified of public speaking for decades. Just the thought of standing up in front of a group of people made her shake, sweat, and feel light-headed. But addressing large audiences was a big part of a new job she had just landed. The root cause of Marcie's terror was an incident in her early childhood when she had been beaten for talking back to her father.

During the MER process, Marcie was able to revisit that painful event, but as if she was watching it happen on a movie screen in the distance. From this position, she was able to release all of the negative emotions from the incident. By the end of the MER session, she could talk about the memory calmly and with no feelings of distress, and she was almost eager to plan her next speaking engagement.

Weeks later, Marcie reported, "Now I feel just a little nervousness that disappears the moment I walk up to the podium. I'm not sure public speaking will ever be my favorite thing to do. But I feel very confident doing it now, and it's opened up several doors that would have stayed closed to me."

From Specific to General

Another benefit of the Mental and Emotional Release technique is that the outcomes generalize automatically to other situations or issues. For instance, Mona not only felt less angry at her mother, she also found that she didn't get angry as easily at her job, with her children, or in traffic. Marcie not only felt more confident speaking to audiences, she also was more comfortable talking about difficult issues with her partner and asking her boss for a raise.

No Relapse

The changes clients experience through MER have shown to be permanent. Unlike some other therapies that require constant oversight or ongoing medication to prevent relapse, once clients make a significant shift in MER, it's done. In my experience of twenty-two years, I've never had a client return complaining of an issue we previously worked with.

Can someone have new problems arise? Of course. But when the technique has been done properly and clients experience a complete release of negative emotions and limiting beliefs, the original issue will not return. And through the release work, clients now have a baseline of mental and emotional health that allows them to deal with new problems more quickly and effectively. MER studies are only a few years old, so they can't point to decades-long results. But I'm confident that follow-up studies down the road will support the longevity of results.

I grew up with these techniques and actually worked with clients by the time I was thirteen. I was a pretty sharp kid, but at that young age, I wasn't working with anything very deep. But one of my very first clients was a breakthrough session (similar to the MER intensive we do today) and actually turned out to be one of the most challenging of my career.

Maybe it was challenging because it was my first "big" one. And looking back, I actually did a really good job. Though when I started, I just thought my client, Lana, was really into her baggage.

Some people identify so much with their baggage that it becomes who they are. "I'm sickly." "I'm unlovable." "I'm the kinda person who never gets a break." Initially, I thought this was Lana. Her aunt was a student of mine who asked if I could work with her niece.

Lana's presenting problem was that she had chronic migraines. I asked for her doctor's referral, and it was recommended that Lana continue with her strong course of medication as I worked with her. Please understand that people can have migraines because of physiological issues. However, migraines often have a mental and emotional component, and this is what I thought I could help Lana with.

As we began the detailed personal history, I found that Lana had a long history of physical issues. As soon as one was relieved, a new one cropped up. Before migraines, Lana had stomach problems. Before the stomach problems, she had back issues. Before the back issues, she experienced joint problems. And before the joint problems, Lana had stress and severe sleeplessness.

Finally, we hit the deeper issue, which shook me to my core. When Lana was a child, her father had kidnapped her. He took her to another state to a cult, where she was ritualistically abused for roughly two weeks. Knowing what I know now as a doctor, her survival skills alone are admirable.

Lana shared with me that she had not told anyone this besides her mother, her aunt, and the police. The rest of the family had no idea, nor did she want them to know. In all honesty, she was shocked that she had even mentioned the event to me. As I pointed out the path of physiological issues stemming all the way back to this period, she realized that the deeper emotional baggage that she carried was making her unhealthy in the physical.

What made this so difficult was the content of Lana's release. This technique can be done content free, but for more complicated issues like this one, you need to delve into the client's history to at least some degree. To be clear, I never had to find out any details of the abuse or the trauma that took place over two weeks in that cult. I simply had to know that Lana's trauma came from that particular event in order to guide her to release it.

Lana had previously seen a therapist about her ordeal and immediately asked, "Do I have to relive all of this again?"

I told her no and then asked, "Are you ready to release it?"

Fighting back tears, she said, "Please, and is there any way you can erase my memory of it?"

I'm glad I didn't have children of my own at this time because it would've probably lit up more baggage in me than I would've been prepared to deal with. But I was able to remain calm and empathetic as I took her through the process of releasing anger, sadness, fear, hurt, and guilt.

This was back in the 1990s. I still tell this story occasionally at trainings, and I still see her aunt on a regular basis. Lana has remained migraine free and hasn't had any more physical symptoms related to her trauma. She was able to enter into a very positive relationship, and she ended up having children. Her aunt often tells me how happy Lana is in her life.

This first initial experience of working with someone with that depth of an issue really shaped my passion and motivation for helping others. I said to myself, "If someone who's been through the closest thing to hell I can imagine can get over their baggage, then anyone can."

In the early days, based on this experience and other client breakthroughs, I had great faith that the technique worked. With new research, we're able to add empirical evidence to that faith.

2

Basic NLP Concepts

Some of you may not be familiar with Neuro Linguistic Programming (NLP). Since MER is based on NLP, I'd like to give you a brief overview of some of NLP's most important concepts so you have a sense of why and how this approach works.

You can learn a lot about NLP simply by looking at its name: Neuro Linguistic Programming.

Neuro refers to the nervous system (the mind) through which all of our experience is processed via the five senses: sight, sound, touch, smell, and taste.

Linguistic refers to language as well as nonverbal communication systems through which our internal representations (memories and beliefs) are coded, ordered, and given meaning. Linguistics includes pictures, sounds, feelings, tastes, smells, and words (self-talk).

Programming refers to the patterns in our neurological systems. It's like the "apps" we carry around in our bodies. With NLP, we have the ability to discover, use, or modify these programs to achieve specific and desired outcomes. Some people have an issue with the word "programming," as if it is some kind of cultish, brainwashing process. I will often say that if we were to create NLP today, we would probably call it "Neuro Linguistic Apps."

In other words, NLP uses the language of the mind to "reprogram" our internal applications to consistently support us in achieving our specific, desired outcomes. A desired outcome might mean success in career, improved relationships, or enhanced physical ability. In a therapeutic context, clients might desire calm and confidence instead of debilitating anxiety, or they might want to feel more even-keeled emotionally rather than constantly battling depression.

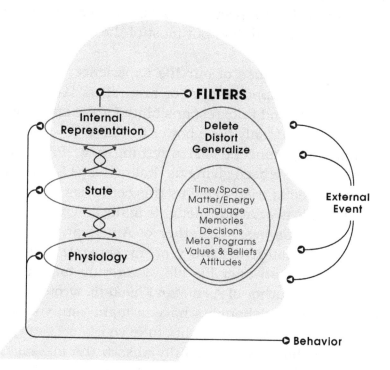

In his books, *Biology of Belief* and *The Honeymoon Effect*, Dr. Bruce Lipton talks about where our programming comes from and techniques that we can use to help overcome this programming. NLP is specifically designed to help people overcome their deepest programming. This programming usually originates before the age of seven, which is referred to as the imprinting phase.

You're the Cause, Not the Effect

One of the basics concepts of NLP is that, at some level, we all have a hand in creating our lives and our experience of life. This isn't to say that we're at fault or should feel guilty if our lives aren't turning out as we want. Few of us consciously choose to screw up our own lives. Few of us consciously choose to feel miserable or procrastinate or hurt others' feelings. Few of us consciously choose to feel angry or fail to meet our goals. We do create our lives and our reactions to life, but most of the creating we do is unconscious.

We are the *cause* of our life experience, not just the effect of what happens to us or around us. And when we recognize this and take responsibility for the effects we are causing, we suddenly have power again.

This whole concept isn't anything new. Philosophers and healers have been giving us that message for centuries. Marcus Aurelius tried to tell us this centuries ago when he said, "Our life is what our thoughts make it." Over 150 years ago, William James, the father of American psychology, said, "The greatest discovery of my generation is that a human being can alter his life by altering his attitudes." James Allen, author of *As a Man Thinketh*, wrote, "You are today where your thoughts have brought you; you will be tomorrow where your thoughts take you."

Yet somehow, we didn't fully absorb the message. For many of us, the notion that we are the architects of our lives is the opposite of what we've been brought up to believe. Commonly accepted thinking in our culture would say that life happens *to* us, and that we're like pawns being played with no choice in the matter, not even much choice over our own emotions or reactions.

But our reactions and emotions are actually based on decisions that we (or more accurately, our unconscious minds) made at very early ages. Take a young child who sees that his mother is frightened by a dog. That young unconscious mind figures, "Uh-oh. Must be something dangerous about dogs." Based on the decision of that moment, the unconscious mind then tees up the fear response whenever dogs are in the vicinity, to remind us to beware. The dog itself did not make us feel fearful. Our own unconscious *decision* about dogs did.

"Your living is determined not so much by what life brings to you as by the attitude you bring to life; not so much by what happens to you as by the way your mind looks at what happens."—Khalil Gibran

We have control over our responses to life, and the source of that control is in our unconscious minds. The good news is that we have a choice, and using techniques of NLP and MER, we can modify any unconscious decisions that don't serve us.

Hannah, a fifty-year-old high school teacher, hated using the phone and did almost anything to avoid making a call. It didn't matter if it was a business or personal call, Hannah shuddered just thinking about speaking on a phone. She'd drive miles out of her way to handle small issues in person, or spend hours drafting letters, all to avoid any interactions on the phone. But when she decided to start her own tutoring business, she knew she needed to get over the issue.

Hannah worked with one of my Master Practitioner students to address the problem and other issues. During the MER process, Hannah recalled an incident from her early teens that turned out to be the root cause of her telephone problem. She said, "I called a friend to ask for a favor, and she flat out yelled at me. I felt horrible and decided then and there that I would never get on the phone to ask for anything ever again." Guided through the MER process by my student, Hannah was able to release all of the negative emotions around that incident, as well as her limiting decision about phones.

In the follow-up session a week later, Hannah said, "Being able to just get on the phone and call someone is so

freeing. I can't believe that I used to drive halfway across town, just to avoid picking up the phone. Life just got much easier."

Perception Is Interpretation

Another core concept of NLP is that perception is interpretation. In other words, what we perceive is more a function of what's happening *inside* of us than what's happening *out there*. Here's how it works:

As an event happens, we take it in via our five senses. But our five senses are picking up over two million bits of information *every second*: way too much to absorb. So our brain filters that two million bits down to a manageable 126 bits[5] by deleting, generalizing, and distorting the input. It does this based on our prior memories, decisions, values, beliefs, and attitudes, which are housed in both the unconscious and conscious mind. That means that we *never* really perceive what happened. We perceive what we expected or understood or believed to have happened.

"Everything we hear is an opinion, not a fact. Everything we see is a perspective, not a truth."—Marcus Aurelius

This isn't so hard to prove to yourself. Have you ever talked about some old childhood event with your siblings (or even better, with your parents) and notice how differently you each remember that event? You remember details differently and undoubtedly ended up with different interpretations or conclusions. It's not because they have faulty memories. It's that you each used your own unique filters to process it.

This is particularly important because that filtered input becomes your internal representation (memory or belief) of the event, which creates a state (emotional response), which affects your physiology, which causes you to behave in a certain way. Take the example of the child who interpreted his mother's fear of dogs as "Dogs

---

5   According to the book *Flow* by Mihaly Csikszentmihalyi.

equal danger." Based on that memory (which he may not even remember consciously), whenever he sees a dog, the emotional state of fear rises up, which tells his physiology to "flee or fight," which then causes him to back away from or prepare to defend himself against the dog. In NLP, when a client wants to stop a negative or limiting behavior, we focus on modifying that internal representation, which then automatically shifts the physiological response, emotional reactions, and behavior.

A student of mine had a young client who ended up in the ER because of an early internal representation. Tim was a sixteen-year-old who had gone hiking with his girlfriend. They came across an injured bird, and the girlfriend wanted to bring it to the vet. Tim had always avoided birds, but he agreed and helped her put the bird in the car.

By the time they got back to town and dropped the bird off at the vet, Tim was having a full-blown panic attack. His heart was racing, and he was having trouble breathing. He felt chilled and reported chest pain. Doctors in the ER checked him out, diagnosed it as a panic attack, balanced his electrolyte levels, and sent him home. Tim knew that the incident stemmed from his terror of that bird.

During his MER session with my student, Tim recalled visiting Central Park as a toddler with his mother. His mom gave him a sandwich and then turned to talk to friend. As she did, Tim was surrounded by pigeons, who pecked at him to get the sandwich. He fell, and the birds flew off with the sandwich. By the time his mother turned around, Tim was on the ground weeping (and was then scolded for bad behavior).

As years passed, Tim had forgotten about the incident. But his fear of birds remained with him. His unconscious mind retained the representation of birds as related to extreme danger. So when he came in close contact with that injured bird, the unconscious triggered the emotional and physiological reaction from the earlier incident as a toddler.

After one MER session, Tim was able to completely release his fear of birds.

Think of a time when you were totally upset about something, only to find out that what you thought had happened, never did. What happens to those very real emotions and physical reactions you had? Or imagine watching someone pounding on another person's chest as they lie on the sidewalk. If you didn't know about CPR, you might get angry at or be frightened of that "attacker." But once you realized it was someone performing a lifesaving measure, your entire perspective would change, and with it your emotional, physiological, and behavioral response.

Energy-Mind-Body Connection

The third basic concept is that we are built with a direct energy-mind-body connection. Again, not a new concept. In fact, until the 1800s, it was commonly accepted that emotions often caused disease. You could "die from a broken heart" or anger could cause your "bile to rise." But as science progressed, doctors discovered other "causes" for illness, like bacteria and toxins or even aging. Many physicians stopped looking at the entire picture of a patient's life to find the holistic root cause of the disease. Instead, they looked only for physical causes of physical ailments and then relied on medication to alleviate the symptoms.

Fortunately, science has progressed further and now recognizes that energy-mind-body are intertwined. Developmental biologists like Dr. Bruce Lipton led the way with books like *Biology of Belief.* Leading universities and hospitals systems now have mind-body research and healing departments. For example, the goal of the Center for Mind-Body Research at John Hopkins is to facilitate "productive interdisciplinary collaborations in mind-body research and to apply innovative research methodologies to elucidate psychobiological mechanisms linking emotional and cognitive processes with health and illness" (which is a big fancy way of just saying, "Let's look at the whole person for healing").

And it's not just the professional community that has renewed interest in the energy-mind-body connection. Katie Couric moderates panels on mindfulness, and *Time* magazine[6] publishes articles about how journaling about trauma can speed up physical healing. Books with titles like *Deadly Emotions: Understand the Mind-Body-Spirit Connection That Can Heal or Destroy You*[7] hit the bestseller lists. Today, every physical therapist, personal trainer, and sports coach talks about the impact our minds have on our bodies. If our emotional and mental "bodies" are not in alignment with healing, physical healing will be delayed (if not prevented).

---

6   *Time* magazine article by Maia Szalavitz, July 13, 2013.
7   By Don Colbert.

Many years ago, I was approached by one of my students after a training. Lisa was a bright professional woman in her thirties. She told me that she previously had breast cancer and now had a new tumor. Her doctors wanted her to begin chemo, but she was seven months' pregnant. Years before, during a prior course of chemo, she had lost a baby, and she was determined not to lose this one.

I coordinated with her doctors, who believed that the MER process could help Lisa reduce her stress, which would help with her healing. During her seven-hour MER breakthrough session, Lisa uncovered several deep fears about having children and emotional issues with her own mother. After the session, she was able to release these fears and issues.

When Lisa went in for her chemo treatment, her doctors performed a scan and discovered that her tumor had shrunk. With only one chemo treatment, the doctors announced that her cancer was once again in remission. A couple months later, she happily delivered a healthy baby girl. Lisa firmly believes that the healing she achieved was possible because of the negative emotions she was able to release.

NLP techniques use this connection, working with our physiology and both our conscious and unconscious minds. It is our bodies and the feelings in our bodies that often tell us what to do, *not* the logic of our conscious minds. Take, for example, the fight, flee, or freeze syndrome: When faced with danger, the sympathetic nervous system immediately prepares the body to defend itself, run, or "hide" by staying frozen. It steps up our heart rate, speeds up our breathing, releases adrenalin and cortisol to the body, and increases blood flow to muscles. And all of this happens whether the danger is real or not. We can even *consciously* know that we're not in danger (like when we're watching a scary movie), but we'll still feel the physical reaction. Remember the example of a child with a fear of dogs? Even as a thirty-year-old, 185-pound man, he might still get freaked by a three-pound Chihuahua.

In NLP, when our physical responses are counter to what we want or what is healthy for us, we work with the unconscious thoughts, beliefs, and internal representations, which in turn modify physical reactions and feelings.

We Are Responsible for Change

Another core concept of NLP is that we and we alone are responsible for making the changes we wish to make in ourselves. No, there's no magic pill or enlightened guru who can do it for us. There *are* practical tools we can use, but we're the ones who have to decide to use them.

This is important. Too many of us have become accustomed to looking out there for the answers. We think of our physicians and therapists like rolling into the auto mechanic's shop: "Just fix it!" But MER practitioners will tell you that they can only *guide* you. They can offer highly effective techniques. But it requires your full participation and willingness for the process to produce your desired outcomes.

This brings up an important point about MER and any NLP techniques: People who are not able to establish rapport with their unconscious minds or who cannot follow a train of thought are *not* candidates for this work. For example, people with thought disorders like schizophrenia or psychosis or the manic side of bipolar would not be able to make the linguistic connections or have the focus needed to succeed with this process. Clients who are on heavy sedation or antipsychotic medications may not have full access to their unconscious minds. Clients with extreme attention deficit disorder (ADD), who are not on medication to help them concentrate, may not be good candidates, either.

On the flip side, children as young as five are excellent candidates for MER. Though they can be distracted and fidgety during the process and have limited intellectual understanding, they are great at "playing the game" and engaging with the techniques. Once children get to the age of eight, they are usually able to handle the technique as it is done with adults.

Nancy, one of my students, is a licensed marriage family therapist and is very gifted at working with kids. In using the MER process, one of the youngest she has worked with was five years old, a little girl we'll call Sarah.

Sarah was having trouble sleeping at night; she suffered from occasional bedwetting, and she seemed sad much of the time. Because this sadness seemed to be contributing to the sleeplessness, Sarah's pediatrician recommended that her parents take her to counseling to assist with the treatment.

Nancy had used MER with older children but wasn't sure if the technique would work with someone so young. She started by having Sarah draw her time line [the time line will be explained in the next chapter] and color in where any bad things had happened along it. To Nancy's surprise, Sarah explained that she was originally sad in her "mommy's tummy." They talked about sadness, and Sarah said that it "wasn't fun to be sad." She was able to grasp that she could just "let it go," so my student ran her through the MER process, and Sarah enthusiastically released her sadness.

Since that session, Sarah's parents report that she is sleeping much better, and the bedwetting has stopped completely.

3

About the Unconscious

Many psychological therapeutic methods work primarily with the conscious mind, whereas NLP and MER works with the *un*conscious mind (aka subconscious mind), the place where our deep-seated beliefs, values, attitudes, and memories reside. Why? Because that's where the majority of our energy and power comes from.

Right or wrong, if our unconscious mind believes that something is impossible for us, it *is* impossible. If our unconscious mind thinks that life is a struggle, it *will* be a struggle for us. If we've got an unconscious memory of a circus clown terrifying us, we may always experience fear around clowns, no matter how we try to rationalize or talk ourselves out of it. Whenever we have a stubborn reaction that is unwanted, we need to work with the unconscious to create lasting change.

During our Master Practitioner trainings, students exchange MER sessions with one another. When Holly was in the role of client, she talked about her strong belief that she wasn't particularly smart, even though she had graduated from Stanford. The student who was acting as practitioner pointed out the obvious logical fallacy of that belief. He reminded her of her accomplishments and her degrees and tried to persuade her that she was wrong. But the furthest Holly would budge from her belief was that maybe she was "smart-ish."

After completing her MER session, Holly felt differently, saying, "Did I say that I wasn't smart? Actually, I'm a kind of a genius. Not in all ways, but in those that count."

In an NLP context, there are a few characteristics of the unconscious mind[8] that are especially important to understand. Why? Your unconscious mind is an incredibly powerful piece of equipment. Even though we weren't given operating manuals for this equipment, we can learn to use it to our great benefit. First, a little background:

Based on current research, the unconscious mind runs roughly 95 to 99 percent of your consciousness, your body, and your mind. The unconscious mind is a much more powerful processor than the conscious mind. Studies on neural pathways show that the unconscious mind controls a greater part of the brain than the conscious mind, and that part of the brain can handle 40 *million* nerve impulses per second. In contrast, the frontal lobe that is controlled by the conscious mind can handle only forty per minute. In other words, your unconscious mind is like a supercomputer, and your conscious mind is like a slide ruler (for those of you significantly younger than I am, let's just say an adding machine or simple calculator).

Prime Directives of the Unconscious

The unconscious mind has certain "prime directives" or primary missions. This is a fancy way of saying the job description of the unconscious. As a Doctor of Psychology, this list and explanation is more for the general public. Some of these points below have textbooks and entire divisions of psychology associated with them. For the purpose of this book, I wanted to keep it simple and illustrate each

---

[8] For more in-depth information about the unconscious mind, order *Integrate the Shadow, Master Your Path* here www. shopnlp.com

concept with tangible examples. Here are a few that are most relevant to working with MER and NLP:

The unconscious mind preserves the body. Because your unconscious mind is determined to protect you and help you survive, it will fight to keep you from anything it perceives to be dangerous to your survival. For example, a woman I worked with had a deep belief that having a sexy body made her vulnerable to predators. With her example, she maintained an unhealthy body in part because she *never* wanted to look sexy. To change this unconscious program, you can either convince the unconscious that a sexy body is safe or persuade the unconscious that what it's doing to keep you unsexy is dangerous to your health. Keep in mind that this change in belief about what's more likely to help you survive must happen on the *un*conscious level, not just the conscious level. For her, this was a major part of the release work that she needed to do. In my own journey, I held onto excess weight for a decade, because of a deep unconscious belief that if people still liked me even though I was overweight, then they are "true" friends.

(Please remember in all these examples, they are not universal experiences, and some people have an opposite reaction to a belief like the ones above. That is what makes the mind so interesting.)

The unconscious mind runs the body. Your physical body is a complicated combination of sophisticated systems running multiple processes in every moment. Scientists now know that it is our unconscious mind that directs all of these processes. In fact, our conscious mind can control only a few of the processes that the body needs to survive (like breathing, and only when you focus on it). Can you consciously control hormone production? Blood flow to your organs? Heart rate? You cannot do those things consciously; however, your unconscious mind can and does.

In NLP, we say that the unconscious mind holds two

blueprints of the body: one as it is now and one that is its blueprint for perfect health. Our very DNA knows what good health is and how to get there. Our bodies are *designed* to be healthy, to repair and heal themselves. So if the unconscious mind is doing something that is *not* healthy, it's doing so for what it considers to be a good reason. For example, if you have allergic reactions to flowering plants in spring, somehow your unconscious mind may have perceived pollens as a threat. It produces watery eyes and running nose to defend you against this "enemy." But once your unconscious mind is convinced that pollens are *not* dangerous, it turns those defense mechanisms off and allows your body to heal.

The unconscious mind is the domain of emotions and communicates through emotions. Your unconscious mind uses your emotions to signal you. For example, if your unconscious mind (based on deep-seated attitudes, beliefs, and values) believes that a certain kind of person would be a good mate for you, you'll *feel* attracted to and infatuated by that kind of person (even if you consciously know they wouldn't be very wise choice). If your unconscious mind believes you might fail at a certain career and that you'd be crushed by that failure, it will signal you with fear to keep you from even trying.

The unconscious also processes and communicates in symbols and images. When your unconscious is trying to alert you to something, it will often do so through imagery, like the imagery in dream states. These images are symbolic rather than literal. For example, many of us dream about going to school without our clothes on or in our pajamas. Your unconscious mind isn't really worried that you'll forget to get dressed in the morning. But it may be concerned that you aren't fully prepared for an activity or that an upcoming situation will leave you too vulnerable.

Because your unconscious processes in images, it doesn't easily process negatives. In other words, if you say,

"I don't want to be late," the initial image your unconscious creates is of you being late. It requires an extra step for your unconscious to translate that desire into "I want to be on time or early." This is why it is much more effective to focus on what you want, *not* on what you don't want.

The unconscious mind organizes and stores your memories. Amazingly, it's all still in there. Even if your retrieval system seems a little weak at times, your unconscious has carefully stored all those decades of detailed input—input that was *filtered and distorted* according to your values, beliefs, attitudes, and other memories.

Your unconscious mind organizes these memories in two ways. One is according to *time*, as in "this happened when you were two" or "that happened when you were twenty." The second organization is by "gestalt" (my apologies to Gestalt therapists out there for our loose definition of the word). A gestalt is an integrated pattern of similar individual happenings that make up a larger whole. For example, your unconscious may group a scolding from your first grade teacher, an argument with your drill sergeant, and a reprimand from a boss together under the heading of Authority Figures. Your six-year-old birthday party, your first kiss, and the birth of your child might be strung together as joyful experiences. It may group all times you felt unloved in one place and any time you succeeded against the odds in another.

This becomes important in the Mental and Emotional Release process because an inappropriately strong reaction to an existing situation may very well stem from prior memories in that same group (or what we call gestalt). Take a woman who has an overwhelming fear of intimate relationships. Most likely, she has built up an entire chain of painful memories under the heading of People Can Hurt Me. An ardent thrill-seeker might have a huge inventory of Fun, Exciting Risks.

The unconscious sometimes represses painful memories. Again, based on its mission to see that you survive, your unconscious may protect you from unresolved negative emotions. It will wait until it thinks you are ready, *or* when the danger of *not* resolving these emotions is greater than the danger of facing them. When it thinks you're ready or the time is right, your unconscious will present these unresolved emotions to your conscious mind so you can deal with them. Often, this happens suddenly and for no apparent reason.

For example, a student of mine had a client who suddenly remembered a traumatizing incident from her past. As a young child, she and her mother took the family's pet dog to be euthanized. Though barely old enough to understand what was happening, she did recognize that her mother was distraught and that something was very wrong. Many years later as an adult, the client wanted to become an obedience trainer and animal communicator, but she was riddled with doubt. At that point, her unconscious mind presented the earlier trauma to her conscious mind for resolution.

Coming full circle from ancient medical practices, modern medicine is beginning to recognize that unresolved painful emotions are held in the body and can cause disease and discomfort. Many physicians now agree with Dr. Edward T. Creagan, an oncologist at the Mayo Clinic, who said, "Unresolved grief can surface years later as headaches, relationship issues, intestinal problems, mental health difficulties, eating disorders, chemical dependency or other issues."[9] In NLP, we believe (along with many in the medical community) that releasing these old wounds and negative emotions assists with physical healing.

The unconscious makes associations and learns quickly. To ensure your survival, the unconscious mind

---

[9]   http://www.qualityhealth.com/depression-articles/dangers-holding-emotions

must stay alert and grab any important lesson from each and every experience. It doesn't have time to analyze each individual experience as something brand new. Instead, it draws on your past experience. It assumes (rightly or wrongly) that this new experience is similar to another in the past and chooses its reactions accordingly. For example, if you have a horrible experience learning your numbers in kindergarten, your unconscious may associate *all* learning experiences together into the "this is going to be horrible" category—including any future experiences. Before you even walk through the classroom door, it will warn you of the difficulty and "danger" of learning by giving you sweaty palms, rapid heartbeat, and feelings of anxiety. On the other hand, if you do well in physical activities as a child, your unconscious might associate all exercise and sports with success and pleasure. Years later, even *thinking* about going for a run or playing a game of tennis will make you feel positive and energized.

The unconscious shares many traits of a seven-year-old. You can think of the unconscious like a seven-year old child who still operates from the same childhood moral code you adopted when you were young. That moral code often sounds like the voice of your parents: "Good girls don't make messes." "Big boys don't cry." "Life's about survival of the fittest." "No one loves a loser." Even though as an adult you may consciously reject the morals of your childhood, your unconscious mind may still cling to them as strong "beliefs." So, for example, a young attorney may recognize she needs to be more assertive to be successful. But if her unconscious belief is "Girls shouldn't be too pushy," she'll find it hard to act more assertively. Her unconscious will resist going against its "moral code" (unless or until that belief is changed on the unconscious level).

Also like a seven-year-old, your unconscious is always trying to please you, and it pays attention to everything you say. If you say, "This job is a pain in the neck," your unconscious may do everything it can to make sure your neck hurts at work. And without very clear direction, it will do what it *thinks* you want. It will pay more attention to and work to support your *repeated* thoughts and actions rather than your infrequent affirmations. That's why spending ten minutes a day affirming "Money flows to me easily and abundantly" is fruitless if you spend the other twenty-three hours and fifty minutes worrying about your finances and recalculating your debt load. Your unconscious mind is throwing all of its power toward maintaining the lack you're obviously more interested in.

The unconscious mind controls and filters all perceptions. As I mentioned earlier, the unconscious mind takes in a tremendous amount of data. To handle that data efficiently, it discards, distorts, and generalizes the input based on previous experience and decisions it made from that previous experience. Only a small bit of this data makes it through this sorting and reconstructing process for you to become conscious of it. You'll actually "see" what you expect to see or even *not* see something that's right in front of you, if it doesn't fit into what you believe to be true.

This has been proven time and time again with eyewitnesses to crime scenes. DNA testing was first introduced in the 1990s. Of 239 convictions the Innocence Project overturned using DNA evidence, researchers reported that 73 percent had been based on erroneous eyewitness testimony, and one-third of those overturned cases had been based on two or more mistaken eyewitnesses who had been sworn to "tell the whole truth and nothing but the truth."[10] These witnesses weren't lying. *They fully believed that they had seen something that wasn't there* due to distortions their unconscious minds made based on their underlying beliefs.

The unconscious mind maintains instincts and

---

[10] http://www.scientificamerican.com/article/do-the-eyes-have-it/

habits. Basic instincts are built into our very DNA to ensure our survival and the survival of our species. Our gut instincts warn us of danger or alert us to opportunity. But for the last several centuries, Western culture has emphasized conscious thought, logic, and evidence-based analyses for decision-making. Because our instincts are beyond our conscious understanding, we tend to override them or ignore their signals. Despite being ignored, the unconscious mind makes sure that these instincts stay intact and continues to try to signal us through emotions and physical sensations.

The unconscious mind also has the ability to create *habits* as an efficient way to navigate the world. A habit is something you do without thinking, and you're often not even aware that you're doing it at the time. Rather than reinventing every small action of your day, your unconscious mind puts many tasks on autopilot, like which shoe you put on first or the act of brushing your teeth before bed. A habit starts as a conscious behavior that you have to think about and decide to do. But with time and repetition, the behavior gets wired into your unconscious. It's a bona fide habit when your unconscious mind is totally in charge of activating this behavior, when you automatically do something a certain way and you just don't feel right when you try to do it differently.

Of course, some habits turn out to be not so helpful, such as eating too much when under stress or always using humor to deflect confrontation rather than dealing with the stressors or chewing on your fingernails when you're nervous. Consciously trying to change an ingrained habit can be tough because the *conscious* mind isn't in charge of it. However, if the change is approached by getting the unconscious mind on board, as with NLP techniques, the unwanted habit can disappear or be modified pretty easily.

A habit might become stronger with repetition, but it can be installed almost instantly. For example, the habit of using an oven mitt may get installed after the very first time you burn yourself on a hot pan.

To change a habit or a habitual way of reacting or to install a positive new habit, the unconscious needs repetition, but it doesn't necessarily need time. In many cases, when an NLP technique is used properly, lasting change can be virtually instantaneous.

Okay, so you now have some understanding of your unconscious mind. Let's simplify it further. In *Integrate the Shadow, Master Your Path*, I use the analogy of an orchestra: The conscious mind is like the conductor who guides the orchestra and determines how a piece should be played. But the music itself comes from the orchestra's musicians and instruments, which is the unconscious mind.

Most everyone knows what a smartphone is, right? Understanding your unconscious mind is like learning how to use your operating system. Whether you like Android or iPhone, you have to learn how to use the basic operating system. Using MER or NLP techniques is like downloading a new app that can modify your operating system to remove any glitches in the system and get it to work the way you want it to.

4

Emotions and Emotional Baggage

[*When I reviewed my first draft of this book, I felt that it needed more on emotions and emotional baggage, especially for readers who have little or no background in psychology. So I enlisted a colleague of mine who specializes in emotional work, Tris Thorp, to write the following section. For over ten years, Tris has taught emotional healing and healthy ways to navigate the world of emotions at the Chopra Center for Wellbeing. I've been so impressed with her work that I recently recruited her to join me in reformatting and co-teaching the Empowering Your Life® trainings. Here's what Tris teaches about emotions.*]

Emotions are often referred to as the language of the heart. They represent our innermost feelings and are one of the ways in which we have learned to associate with ourselves, other people, and experiences. As human beings, we are meant to experience and express the full range of our emotions, from the saddest to the happiest, from the angriest to the most loving, and everything in between. When we suppress our emotions due to the feelings of discomfort they generate, we disable an aspect of ourselves that we need to be whole.

Learning to understand what emotions are, where they come from and how they become imprinted, how they lead to the labels we use, and the stories we create is paramount if we ever hope to attain any level of holistic integration and enlightenment.

My definition of enlightenment is simply to lighten up, to let go of anything that isn't 100 percent necessary for the journey that lies ahead. Think about it: If you're getting ready to embark on a trek through the Himalayas, are you going to pack an old, worn-out pair of sneakers that are falling apart? Or are you going to pack a solid pair of hiking boots made of weather-proofed material with great arch support? Are you going to tote your old photo albums that weigh ten pounds, or are you going to save the weight for carrying water and food?

Similarly, you don't want to pack old, worn-out emotions that aren't meant for your journey. Emotions are a gift. They not only make our wonderful moments more wonderful, they can also be our early-warning signals of being off-track and the motivational fire we need to get moving toward our goals. They help us respond appropriately to others and take effective action in situations we encounter. But negative emotions and emotional baggage from the past sabotage the gifts our emotions could give us.

How? By distorting, clouding, and directing our reactions and actions in the present. It's the baggage that you carry into that new relationship or new job. It's the unwanted and unwarranted emotion you might feel on a daily basis, like road rage, fear of being around people, or self-doubt. Rather than experiencing fresh emotions that are appropriate in the present situation, the chain of past negative emotions shows up to limit your ability to act and feel the way you want to get what you desire.

How can you tell if you have old negative emotions that need to be released? This story Dr. Matt told me about his own life is a great example:

Back in 1993, I was attending an NLP Master Practitioner class that my father was teaching. He started talking about his divorce from my mother (they had divorced when I was about five) and how bad their marriage had been. I got so upset and enraged that I had to walk out of the room, ranting to myself, Why hadn't he told me this? Why did he have to bad mouth Mom in front of all these people?

The co-trainer followed me out and asked what was up. When I told him what I was feeling, he said, "It might be appropriate to react to your dad sharing this. But you know that you have baggage when your reaction is out of proportion to the current external incident." He took me through a quick Time Line process (forerunner of MER), and the anger simply melted away.

Dr. Matt told me that was a real Aha! moment for him. He clearly experienced the difference between feeling emotions that are valid based on the present situation and those that are overblown and unwarranted. Within minutes, he went from a murderous rage to feeling at ease and okay about his dad and the situation. In fact, he and his dad ended up having dinner together that evening and had an easy, totally comfortable discussion about his parents' divorce.

When negative emotions from the past are not released, they create these unwarranted emotions (emotions that are out of proportion to the situation). Take the example of road rage: It might be reasonable to experience some irritation at being cut off in traffic. But to feel a murderous rage and fury? Probably not. A little nervousness about a new job? Of course, most of us might feel a little nervous, along with excitement. But to feel debilitating panic or fear? Odds are those emotions are linked to prior events and unconscious decisions that no longer serve you.

We've all had the experience of naturally releasing old negative emotions. Just think of something that you used to fear that no longer frightens you. For example, maybe as a young child, you were afraid of the dark in your bedroom at night and "the monster hiding under the bed." It's pretty common. But as adults, most of us naturally grew out of that fear. We can still remember that we had it as kids, but the feeling itself is no longer attached to the memory. We don't feel afraid again whenever we think of being a kid going to bed. Adults who have not released that fear—who still feel panic even remembering being that child—will find that the old emotions have infected other areas of their life as well. They may feel generally not safe or unreasonably on edge, even in a familiar, protected environment.

Without releasing our emotional baggage through a process like MER, we can't experience the gift that our emotions are meant to be. Much of my work is focused on helping people tap the power and gift of their emotions. As central as emotions are to our lives and well-being, few of us are ever taught about what emotions really are and how they work. So I'll cover some basics about emotions, with particular focus on negative emotional baggage and how emotions become limiting beliefs about ourselves and our story of who we are and what we're capable of.

Emotions Are Energy in Motion (E-motion)

Everything is made up of energy, and at the deepest level, emotions are energy in motion. This is one of the most valuable concepts I can share when it comes to emotions. Why? Because if emotions are simply energy in motion (as is everything, by the way), that tells us emotions are transmutable; they change form. This may not sound all that profound. But think about it: Don't most people think they *are* their emotions? How often have you heard (or said), "*I am* depressed" or "*I am* afraid" or "*I am* ashamed" or "*I am* hurt" or "*I am* so angry"?

But we are *not* our emotions. We have them or feel them. We feel an emotion for the moment or an hour (okay, so sometimes a lot longer) as a result of some experience we have. The emotion is real and can even be overwhelming. But it only lives for a period of time, and then it fades. Emotions are the energetic, felt perception of thoughts that we associate with feelings in our body. Emotions are energy in motion. And the energy of emotion can change in an instant, whether or not we consciously try to change it.

Have you ever been in a great mood and walked into a room where someone else was grumpy? Did you notice how that person's emotional state immediately had a dulling effect on your own mood? Can you recall a time when you were feeling sad but when your favorite song came on the radio, you felt your mood shift to be more positive? How long did it take for this shift to happen? Almost immediately, right? The energy of emotion can shift without us putting forth any effort whatsoever. This is our unconscious mind at work.

Emotions in their pure state come and go, flowing easily like all energy flows. And since emotions are nothing more than felt energy in motion, we also have the ability to consciously choose to *change* our emotional state in any given moment. But when present emotions are driven by emotional baggage from the past, they don't shift so easily, and we often don't feel like we have control over them. We don't have our emotions at that point—*they have us.*

Who has emotional baggage? We all do. Unless you've done some work to release the primary negative emotions of anger, sadness, fear, hurt, and guilt, they are affecting your present emotional life to some extent—and probably more than you realize.

Two of the most common questions I get from my students are, "How did this all happen?" and "How did I get this way?" These are great questions. Like anything else, it's a process, and the process is relatively simple to understand. In a nutshell:

- We experience an event through our senses, then >
- The experience generates a feeling, which then >
- Becomes a thought or judgment that this feels "good" or "bad" or "safe" or "scary," which leads to >

- An energetic impulse that releases chemicals and intensifies the feelings, causing >
- Our brain to associate that thought and that experience with that feeling.

All this is well and good if the feelings associated to the experience are positive. If every time we see a sunrise, we feel happy or every time we snuggle into bed, we feel safe, that's rarely a problem. Some of our negative emotional associations can be helpful as well, such as feeling uneasy when we're dishonest or uncomfortable when we have hurt someone.

The Emotional Imprinting Process

The primary imprinting phase is from birth to the age of seven. As infants and young children, we are sponges. We take in every sight, every sound, every smell, every taste, every touch, and every sensation. We begin forming internal representations (which are like snapshots in our mind, complete with feelings, sounds, smells, etc.) of what we perceive as good or bad and right or wrong long before we have even learned how to speak. This is also the time when our values are being formed, that internal representation of what is encoded in our unconscious mind as being the most important to us in any given area of our life.

The basis of who we are and how we perceive the world is formed at this time. Significant emotional events during this period certainly contribute a great deal to our emotional makeup. Yet, in both my personal and professional experience, it's often the seemingly insignificant emotional events that leave the biggest marks.

One day when I was in the first grade, I excitedly raised my hand when the teacher asked the class a question. I was certain I had the best answer, the right answer, and I could barely maintain myself as I waited to be called on. Her eyes scanned the room and stopped as she saw me squirming in my chair. "Yes, Tris?" she asked.

Then it happened. The answer I was so certain was right was *wrong*. I felt my heart sink and the blood drain from my face. The other children began to laugh at me. I felt so embarrassed, I wanted to run from the room and never come back. From that point forward, I never again raised my hand in a classroom for fear of being wrong and looking like an idiot.

As an adult, I had completely forgotten about this experience. I didn't even remember this incident until I went through the MER process. What seems like such an insignificant experience was actually where I developed the belief that I wasn't smart enough, which turned into an unconscious commitment to never again put myself out there in front of people. I decided I wouldn't even bother trying anymore.

Emotions give power to our interpretations and make them more solid. Look at your own experience: When you make a decision or have an opinion about something that doesn't really matter to you, how easy is it to change that decision or opinion? Fairly easy, right? But what if you make a decision or form an opinion about something that you're passionate about? Something that you love or hate or that terrifies you? How easy is it to change your mind then? When an event—significant or insignificant—is accompanied by strong emotion, it has a more lasting impact on us.

Even as newborns, we start to interpret what our senses take in. There are two types of interpretations: positive and empowering or negative and disempowering. If the experience we have is positive, we create an internal representation that is positive, like joy and happiness, safety and security, or confidence and pride. If the experience is negative, we'll create one that might include pain and suffering, confusion and frustration, or danger and threat.

Even at this preverbal stage, we connect our feelings to this internal representation.

As Dr. Matt mentioned in the previous chapter, our unconscious minds are incredibly fast learners. Even as infants, we are beginning to sort and filter experiences as positive or negative, safe or unsafe. Our mind is wired to understand our experiences. Evaluating is the process by which we consider and decide how to classify our experiences. In this phase, we begin to evaluate what happened and gauge it as being good-bad, right-wrong, happy-sad, scary-safe. If the experience is traumatic or disempowering in some way, our assessment of the situation will be negative, and we will make it mean something unfavorable about ourselves, other people, or the world we live in.

Anytime we have an experience of something, we filter what we perceive through our existing internal representations: Is this experience good or bad, right or wrong, scary or safe? We associate our experience with an internal representation and begin to interpret and give meaning to our experiences. This is our way of decoding or understanding what is happening.

The Power of Labels

As a baby, you're crawling around, and you bump into something, and you have an emotion. Then something else happens, and you have an emotion. Then, at some point, you have another experience of a previous emotion, and it's reinforced. At some other point, someone tells you, "You look angry," and you now have a label to associate with the feeling. We group our emotions together by experience, then the label represents the experience, so each time we have another experience, we now know what to call it.

As soon as we're old enough, we'll slap labels onto our experiences so that we can categorize them appropriately. The label we give something is what assigns it a specific meaning.

As a toddler, you may have witnessed your parents shouting at one another. You probably felt frightened and perceived this experience as being scary. You then interpreted it to mean that shouting is a threat to your safety. You began to mold yourself into who you think you needed to be to avoid confrontation because "confrontation equals danger and is a threat to survival." As you got older, you might label shouting as "being hostile and aggressive."

Or maybe as a toddler, you witnessed your parents yelling at one another, but then they quickly calmed down and made peace. You might have felt frightened at first but then quickly felt safe again. You might have interpreted this to mean that shouting is no big deal, just a way to get heard. You learned to raise your voice to get what you want. As you got older, you may have labeled shouting as "being assertive."

Can you see how based on your interpretation and the label you give the experience you would end up approaching life differently? You would have assigned a totally different meaning to shouting based on your experience and the labels you used.

Creating a Gestalt of Emotions

One event might have an impact, but a *series* of events that are given the same interpretation becomes powerful. With each event, the negative (or positive) emotional residue attaches to our interpretation and is further reinforced through subsequent similar events as time goes on.

This is how we go about creating the inventory of our memories and beliefs. This series of experiences has created a gestalt, a unified theme of similarly linked emotions and experiences. As Dr. Matt mentioned earlier, in the MER process, we look for the very first of these similar experiences. This first incident may not (in fact, usually does not) look all that dramatic or significant. Yet this one is the root cause, the first time that particular emotion was linked to an event based on your interpretation. This first time sets the pattern for how subsequent similar events will be interpreted and the emotions they will elicit.

For example, what if as a little child, you are teased by other kids on the playground? It doesn't feel good, and you might feel angry or sad. As you feel these feelings, you try to make sense of why is this happening. You decide it means that you aren't good enough, that there is something wrong with you, or that nobody likes you. As a child, you feel confused and heartbroken. You label this as *rejection.*

Then as a teenager or young adult, your first love dumps you for someone else, and you feel like someone has smashed a sledgehammer into your heart. In your heartache, confusion, and pain, you interpret it to mean that your first love never really loved you and, once again, that you aren't good enough and maybe something is wrong with you. You label this as *rejection* and *betrayal.*

As an adult, you don't get the job or promotion you really wanted. You feel sadness, frustration, maybe anger. You perceive the experience as more of the same thing happening to you and interpret it to mean that you're never going to be good enough, that there is something fundamentally wrong with you, or that no one sees your true value. You will likely file this away under the label: *rejection* or *not good enough.*

Once you've labeled an experience and given it meaning, and especially after you've established a series of similar events and interpretations, you have created the heaviest load in your emotional baggage: your limiting beliefs and decisions, or what I call "unconscious commitments."

Limiting Decisions, Beliefs, and Unconscious Commitments

These decisions, beliefs, and commitments keep you from being, doing, or having what you truly want in your life. You might be aware of some of these decisions and completely unaware of others.

What we consider a negative emotion is simply energy that has gotten stuck. This energy represents a time in our lives when something happened and our needs were not met. At this point, negative emotions got lodged, and a belief was generated. Limiting beliefs can result from significant emotional events. But surprisingly, more often than not, they are created by everyday not-so-significant events that your unconscious mind believed to be important. Limiting beliefs and decisions can be imposed upon us by family, friends, peers, or society as a whole. Sometimes, we just take it upon ourselves to adopt them. Basically, they're waiting in every crack and lurking around every corner for us to claim them.

Something happens, and once we've deemed the experience as bad or wrong, we make it mean something negative about ourselves or others. It now becomes a limiting belief: "I'm not good enough. I'm not pretty/handsome enough. No one appreciates me. I'm not smart enough. I will never have enough. They like her/him more than me. I will always be alone." Any of this sound familiar?

In each of these cases, what preceded the limiting belief was the decision—conscious or unconscious—to take on the belief. You *decided* to believe that failing the math test meant that you were stupid. You *decided* to believe that having a differently shaped body meant that you were unattractive. You *decided* that they must like her better than you. You *decided* to believe that being left by someone you love meant that you weren't worthy of love. Understanding this very subtle yet highly important detail allows you to see where you made the decision, consciously or unconsciously, to adopt these beliefs.

In some cases, we take it even further by making an unconscious commitment to being a certain way, doing specific behaviors, and running behavior patterns to reinforce our beliefs. In the emotional imprinting phase, this is how we self-install a strategy for how we will handle ourselves and recurring situations in life.

Most of us don't realize that we make commitments to ourselves other than the ones we're consciously aware of. You have no recollection of making these unconscious commitments, yet they are what you're most committed to. These unconscious commitments create certain recurring themes in your life. They drive your thoughts and behaviors and create your reality. In other words, they are the culprit that creates the disparity between what you say you want and what you are actually experiencing.

Let's take a step back for a moment to examine how unconscious commitments work using the metaphor of the conscious and unconscious mind, operating like a laptop computer. Envision that, deep within your psyche, you're running your very own operating system. This operating system is programmed to run in specific ways and will only perform as is programmed until old software has been deleted and a new operating system or application has been installed.

Unconscious commitments are a big part of the internal programming that makes up our operating system. When we have some sort of painful or difficult experience in our childhood, we form a limiting decision or belief and create an unconscious commitment as our way of coping. We forget that we ever made the commitment consciously, but it remains embedded in our internal operating system.

The crazy, cool thing is that we originally made the commitment as a way of keeping ourselves safe on some level. Even as young children, we already had some ability for deductive reasoning. "If this equals that, then not-this equals not-that." At the unconscious level, we already figured out that we could avoid embarrassment, ridicule, abuse, rejection, or danger by behaving in a different way. We learned precisely how to avoid potential fall-out from others. This is the power of the unconscious mind. Even as young children, it's at work for us—and working hard, I might add—to protect us from anything that might harm us or interfere with our ability to function in society.

As we continue along the path of life, those old, unconscious commitments are still at work, but now they've most likely become detrimental to our ability to find personal success and fulfillment. The strategies developed by a five-year-old don't necessarily work well for a fifty-year-old. They inhibit us from being the person we are meant to be and limit us from doing the things we want to do. They keep us stuck in a victim mentality, preventing us from having the things we truly want to have.

Here are some examples of unconscious commitments:

"I'll stay quiet so I won't be called stupid."

"Nobody's going to tell me what to do."

"I'll hide my feelings so that I won't be ridiculed."

"I'll stay small and hidden because the world isn't safe."

Now here's where it gets really interesting: Repetitive experiences, day after day after week after month after year, serve to reinforce our beliefs and strengthen our unconscious patterns. We think of it all as a recurring theme that happens to us. But in truth, we *attract and create* these similar situations through our unconscious commitments and limiting beliefs.

How many times have you found yourself in a similarly toxic relationship or working for the same type of overly demanding boss? How many times have you been rejected or taken advantage of by friends or been undervalued in your jobs? You might have spent countless hours wondering why the same-old, same-old keeps happening over and over again.

The answer is quite simple: First, as Dr. Matt teaches in his MER and NLP trainings, a function of the unconscious mind is to create experiences based on your beliefs. What you carry in your unconscious becomes your reality. So in other words, you will attract people and situations that are in alignment with your beliefs. This is because like energies attract like energies.

Say you have a core belief that all men have anger issues because your dad was angry and your grandfather was angry. When you meet a new man, the moment they look agitated, you interpret that as meaning they have anger issues, labeling current events based on past experiences. If your mother had an affair and your teenage girlfriend was unfaithful, you might have developed a belief that all women cheat. You watch a series of movies where women are lying and cheating, which reinforces your belief that dishonesty is universally true in women. Then, when your wife receives a text message from another guy, you might automatically assume that she is betraying you.

Along with misinterpreting, you're also inviting and attracting the same kinds of people, circumstances, and events into your life. Remember that whatever we believe at the unconscious level is what we are most committed to manifesting.

Our unconscious mind naturally goes looking for similar patterns and comparable experiences to validate our beliefs. For example, as a little girl, I believed that my parents didn't want me. Over time, I adopted the belief that I'm not good enough and that everyone I love will eventually leave me. So guess what kinds of romantic relationships I attracted?

I became a pro at manifesting relationships where I was put on the back burner or where our relationship wasn't the focus of my partner's attention. They were leaving all the time, being unfaithful, and writing it off as my being crazy in the head. Truth be told, I *was* crazy in the head by this point because I'd been doing the same thing over and over again my whole life while expecting a different result. Isn't that what they say is the definition of insanity?

What we go looking for, we are sure to find. If we are

attuned to think or behave in certain ways, or we're looking for things in life to be a certain way, we will attract "like" energy and see it reflected back to us. Our unconscious mind then validates our beliefs and creates our reality by continuously attracting similar people, circumstances, and events throughout the course of our lives.

Creating Our Story

Our stories are a composite of our core values, past experiences, emotions, beliefs, personas, and a series of patterns and themes that we continue to repeat unconsciously. Our stories only become real because we have repeated the experiences so many times, it's now become who we think we are. Our stories are the end result of an accumulation of experiences, and our stories are what we take into every role we play.

We share some aspect of our story in every conversation, every friendship, every intimate relationship, every job we take. Every thought we have, every word we speak, and every action we take (or don't take) is an expression of how we interpret ourselves, others, and the world we live in. This is how we create our reality.

Our story is a compilation of fragmented memories, unreconciled negative emotions, and limiting beliefs; it's our track record for recreating similar experiences time and time again. We live our story, and we retell it to ourselves and others in some way every single day, through thoughts, words, actions, and behavior. Naturally, we begin to think that we *are* our stories. It makes logical sense, doesn't it, that we would be that story, since it's on a continual loop?

At some point, we wake up to the idea that our story may be anchoring us to a reality we no longer want to be living. When we are willing to extract ourselves from the Iago trance we've been living in and consciously choose to look at the choices we are making in our lives, we take the first steps toward empowering our lives. We realize that we are the author and the narrator of our life story, and we can choose to make the next chapter more positive, more inspiring, more fulfilling, and, ultimately, more empowering.

How Mental and Emotional
Release Therapy Works

So now that we have a clearer idea about emotions from Tris, let's look at how this technique works. MER is based on how our systems already operate. We've all experienced the release of a negative emotion. We all have things that we were once upset about that no longer concern us. I can't imagine anyone reading this book and thinking, "Nope. I'm still totally upset about everything that ever happened to me."

So it's clear that our unconscious mind knows how to release negative baggage. MER simply uses the unconscious mind's process, its internal storage process of memories and the encoding of these memories into emotions, to get at the root of the problem and release the baggage that you have consciously decided to release. In other words, it works based on how you already operate.

The Goal of MER
In working with the Mental and Emotions Release technique, the goal is to release unresolved negative emotions and the limiting beliefs that hold us back from what we desire. The process itself uses our memories—both conscious and unconscious—to release the emotional charge attached to them. The memory itself isn't erased or necessarily

forgotten. The memory remains. But when clients think of that past event again, they no longer feel the strong negative emotions that were once attached to it.

The goal of MER therapy is not to become emotionless. We will always have emotions, as Tris explained in chapter 4, and some of them will be negative. But by releasing past emotions, whatever emotions we feel in the present will be appropriate the present situation, not colored or exaggerated by an unresolved emotion from the past. And they will tend to disappear or change more quickly. For example, you will still feel grief over a major loss, but that grief will dissipate naturally rather than hang on.

A student of mine was sexually abused as a young child. She thought she'd come to resolution with that event through her forgiveness work. But in her thirties, she recognized how anxious she felt whenever she received unwanted attention from men, even men she knew to be safe. She said, "I had a fear of just saying 'no' to them. So I'd perfected the Ice Queen façade where, if men looked interested in me, I would act as if they didn't even exist." Even though she was single and wished to be in a relationship, she found herself becoming more and more cold and aloof toward men in general.

Through the MER process, she released the panic and fear of that traumatic childhood memory. As a result, she no longer felt the need to keep her guard up. She could relax and enjoy interacting with the men in her life and trusted that she could distinguish between situations that were safe and those that were not safe.

To work with the Mental and Emotional Release process effectively, practitioners are trained to incorporate several components. Each is important for the process to be successful.

Primary Negative Emotions

One of the keys to a successful MER process is to first release the primary negative emotions that everyone experiences: anger, sadness, fear, hurt, and guilt. As those primary emotions are released, clients are often aware of other negative emotions such as shame, hopelessness, or jealousy. We follow the same technique to release those as well. (Anxiety is treated differently because it is an emotion based on future projections of an unwanted result, as opposed to past reactions to an event.)

It's important to honor whatever negative emotions the client's unconscious mind presents, as illustrated in this example:

One of my students worked with a middle-aged client (we'll call Mitchell), who had a relatively successful career as a contractor. Mitchell's goal for the MER sessions was to overcome his constant self-doubts, along with the indecisiveness and procrastination they led to. His overarching issue was "I don't have what it takes to get what I want." After releasing the five major negative emotions, Mitchell noticed that "embarrassment" came to the fore. He had been embarrassed by his father's drinking as a child, embarrassed by having to repeat the fourth grade, embarrassed when he was fired from his first job.

My student later commented, "'Embarrassment' isn't that strong a word to me, so I kept asking if Mitchell meant 'shame.' But I quickly came to understand that 'embarrassment' was incredibly painful for him. Once the emotion of embarrassment was released, the vast majority of his other issues disappeared." By the end of the session, Mitchell felt fully confident and capable, and he eagerly set new goals for his business that he'd not felt were possible for him before.

Today, it's common knowledge that unresolved negative emotions create a multitude of problems. They cause us to react in ways we don't want to react. Holding onto negative emotions casts a shadow that blocks us from experiencing happiness and satisfaction in our lives. If you're feeling a consistent undercurrent of anger or sadness, how likely are you to really enjoy your child's achievements or a beautiful sunset? They sabotage our goals, as with Mitchell's hesitancy to move forward in his career, and can ruin our relationships, as in the example of my student who froze rather than interact with men.

And now there is more and more evidence that unresolved emotions cause health issues. Anger has been associated with heart attacks and high cholesterol. Sadness is linked to suppressed immune systems, and fear leads to excessive stress, which contributes to high blood pressure and diabetes. Studies on guilt and shame indicate that these persistent feelings can increase pro-inflammatory cytokine activity,[11] and inflammation has been linked with illnesses ranging from heart disease, diabetes, and cancer to depression, Alzheimer's, and osteoporosis.

So whether these unresolved emotions are apparent in our lives, as with PTSD or phobias, or not that obvious, it's definitely valuable for us to release them.

In Mental and Emotional Release therapy, we work with the primary negative emotions individually and in a specific order: anger then sadness then fear then hurt then guilt. We've learned to do this because these emotions seem to reveal themselves in this order. When anger is released, it unearths sadness. When sadness dissipates, fear usually appears. When we've dealt with fear, hurt shows up, followed by guilt. Even if a client says that she doesn't really feel one of these emotions, we run the technique on that emotion anyway. Often an emotion is present *un*consciously, even though the client isn't aware of it consciously. If it remains unreleased, that emotion continues to mask the other emotions.

Clients have different responses to the release of these emotions. Anger and fear are stimulant emotions, flooding the body with sensations in the same way a drug stimulant would. So often, after releasing anger or fear, clients will

---

[11] http://www.ncbi.nlm.nih.gov/pubmed/14747646

feel less energized, maybe even down. On the other hand, sadness, hurt, and guilt are depressive emotions, so clients may feel a burst of energy or enthusiasm after releasing those two. Immediately after the release itself, clients might feel happy, almost giddy. Or they might feel flat, a kind of "so what?" feeling. Or they might immediately feel the next primary emotion, for instance, they might feel sadness after releasing anger.

Rapport with the Unconscious Mind

To be effective with the Mental and Emotional Release technique, or any NLP technique, the practitioner and client must first establish rapport with the unconscious mind. What does that mean?

Many of us, especially in Western cultures, are taught to ignore the signals and messages of the unconscious mind. We feel sleepy, but rather than resting as our unconscious would like us to, we push ourselves to keep going. We have a hunch that a certain job or relationship is not good for us. But rather than listening to that hunch, we ask our buddies or mentors what we should do and then follow their advice. Our unconscious mind generates dreams every night. But rather than pausing to understand the message of these dreams, we shake them off and ignore whatever wisdom the unconscious mind is trying to share.

As we discussed in chapter 3, the unconscious mind is a mighty faculty, with more influence over our lives and our outcomes than most of us realize. If we operate only from our conscious minds, it's like unplugging ourselves from our best power source. Our efforts to change or to achieve our goals become difficult or even impossible.

When working with NLP and the MER process, we make sure the unconscious mind is on board with any changes the client consciously wants to make. We build rapport and open up communication with the unconscious by respecting the amazing job it does for us and by honoring its positive intentions for us. The unconscious mind knows where all the bodies are hidden, so we trust it (not the conscious mind) to point out significant events and memories to be released. We also communicate in its language—images, emotions, and symbols—and pay special attention to its signals and feedback throughout the process. For example, if a client's unconscious mind is reluctant to give up anger because anger has worked as a protective mechanism, we help the unconscious develop an alternative strategy to use as protection.

Time Lines and Memories

I mentioned that one of the primary jobs of the unconscious mind is to store and organize memories, and one of the ways it organizes these memories is in time sequence. In a sense, your unconscious mind creates an internal time line of all of your experiences, like a personal file system, so that it can retrieve these memories when needed.

This time line stretches from your past to your future and can appear in a variety of ways. But because we live in a linear world, most of us have some sort of linear time line. Some of us have time lines that are in front of us with the past in one direction and the future in the other. A time line can be from left to right or right to left. Others have time lines that run through their bodies: The past stretches out behind them, and the future stretches before them (or vice versa). Some people have time lines where the past comes from the lower left and the future heads out to the upper right, or the line can form a V-shape or other type of angle.

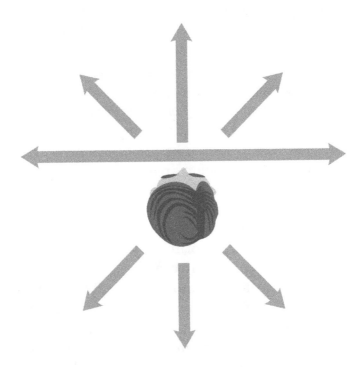

Though the specific configuration of your time line has some meaning to a skilled NLP practitioner, for our purposes here, it's just enough to realize that we all have one and that we can use it in the MER process to access memories to release negative emotions and limiting decisions.

I'm often asked if the memories in this time line are accurate. The answer is yes and no. They are accurate from the point of view that this is the precise memory—with all its emotions, decisions, and conclusions—that your system believes, reacts to, and operates from. Are they accurate factually? It really doesn't matter.

For example, I once worked with a student who believed that he "remembered" hearing his parents argue about money while he was in the womb. Was that factually true? Hard to say. But the important point was that his unconscious mind believed in this memory, had negative emotions about it, and had drawn conclusions about life based on it. It wasn't important to prove or disprove that the event happened. It was important to release the charge and decisions of that stored memory.

Find Your Own Time Line

You may have a sense of how your time line is configured. But if not, there's very simple exercise to discover your own time line. As you do this, be sure to accept the first thing that comes to you. That will be the response from your unconscious mind. If you overanalyze or overthink it, your conscious mind takes over and will confuse the process.

Just relax, and simply think of a specific event from a week ago. As you think of that event, where is it in relation to your body? Go ahead and point to it. Next, think of a specific event from a month or more ago. Where is that memory? Is it farther away from your body? Now think about something that will be happening next week. Where is that event? Point to it. Think about something that is a year or more in the future. Where is that future event? If you draw a line from your past events to your future events, you have your time line. (By the way, a time line doesn't have to be visual. For many people, it's a *sense* of where their past memories and future possibilities are located.)

The Gestalt of Emotions

Again, my apologies to any Gestalt therapists who may be reading this, because we use the term "gestalt" very loosely here. In MER and NLP, as Tris explained in chapter 4, we think of a gestalt as a chain of events that are linked together by the unconscious mind. This is how the unconscious mind learns efficiently, by associating similar events to one another.

As mentioned in chapter 3, to do its job and make sure that you survive, the unconscious mind can't take the time to treat each new experience as totally unique. It hears tires screeching, sees a horrible car crash, and concludes that screeching tires mean "Danger!" The next time it hears screeching tires, the unconscious mind won't stop and wonder if this sound means something else. It will activate your flight response by pumping up your adrenaline and getting you to safety.

But the unconscious mind doesn't always end up with helpful conclusions, and it may apply extreme emotions from one event to other events down the line. For example, a student of mine had a client who had been put into a special program when she was in the third grade because she was behind in reading skills. Twice a week, she felt deep shame when she was called out of the classroom to be tutored. From this experience, she concluded that she "just wasn't as smart as other people." Decades later, in her mid-fifties, this belief and that old sense of shame still ran her life, causing her to reject opportunities and even promotions in her career.

The unconscious connects each event to a similar event preceding it and the next similar event after it. For therapeutic purposes, this connection is extremely useful because if you dislodge the emotions and conclusions from the first one in the chain, you can dislodge the emotions and conclusions in subsequent events. It's like a row of dominoes; when you tip one over, it knocks over the others, and they fall. When the client above released the shame and conclusion she had drawn from her third-grade experience, she was able to recognize her own intelligence and abilities, which freed her to move forward in her career.

Root Cause
The key to completely releasing negative emotions and limiting beliefs is to catch that *very first* domino, and this is where many therapeutic processes fall short. Many therapists are taught to deal with the presenting problem or the significant traumatic events that the client can *consciously* pinpoint. In the row of dominoes, this is rarely

the root cause or initial event. If you work with an event that is down the line from (i.e., happening after) the real root cause, symptoms may subside or even disappear for a short time. But they eventually crop up again. So a therapist may help a client work through one incident of extreme anger. But odds are, in the next session, a different incident of extreme anger will pop up. Then another, and another, ad infinitum. That's why clients can spend months or even years in therapy and never feel quite done with their original issue.

But when you work with the root cause, it's like cutting off the end of a strand of pearls. All the rest of the pearls are going to fall away.

The root cause is the *initial* event which, once it is disconnected, will cause the problem to disappear. More often than not, clients do not even remember this initial event. If they do remember it, it may seem particularly insignificant or even silly to them on the conscious level. However, the unconscious mind can be trusted to find the real root cause event, no matter how unimportant it may appear.

For the major negative emotions, the root cause will have happened no later than the imprinting phase, which is from birth to seven years old. The root cause of specific limiting decisions can be later. Depending on the client's orientation and belief system, the root cause might even be prior to birth, in a past life or via a genealogical connection with their ancestors.

The most important point is that it's the *unconscious* mind, not the conscious mind, which knows exactly where the root cause lies. Both practitioner and client must trust that the unconscious mind knows what it's doing.

A student of mine exchanged MER sessions with another student, Keiko, who had immigrated to the United States from Japan with her parents when she was quite young. Keiko was in her forties, and though she had been successful in business, she now wished to focus on the artistic talents she'd had in her youth. But whenever Keiko tried to paint or sculpt, she felt blocked and inhibited.

In asking about the root cause for the negative emotions and limiting decisions, Keiko was often led to events that had happened generations ago. "I don't know how these things could be passed down through genealogy," she said, "but I've always felt a strong connection to my ancestors." During the process, Keiko was sometimes consciously aware of the event in past generations, but other times, she was not. But when the emotions or decisions of the root cause event were released, she felt her self-consciousness disappear completely, and she was able to express herself fully through her art again.

We call it the root cause, because like the root of a weed, if you want the entire weed gone, you need to kill it from the root. So with MER, we are first exploring how to get to the root cause so that we can release the entire gestalt of the negative emotion we are focusing on.

Visualization

During MER, we ask clients to float above their time line (with their unconscious mind) and notice an event there. Clients often mention that they aren't visual and don't see anything. Some people are more kinesthetic in the process, and others are more auditory. The very first time I did this process, I didn't see my time line. Rather, I experienced feeling the emotions and sensing the memories. Many people I've worked with do not see their time line visually. Therefore, doing the process as visual, auditory, or kinesthetic is fine.

Or putting it in an even easier light to understand, one can just imagine the process. In a sense, it's similar to imagining something. If you imagine being on a tropical island or being with a loved one, you might experience it visually or using your other senses. But however you do it, you know that you are imagining whatever it is.

Disassociation/Association

MER (and other techniques in NLP) use both association and disassociation at certain times for specific reasons. The difference between the two has to do with your relationship to a memory. When you are associated to an event, you see it through your own eyes. You experience the sensations and sounds as if it is really happening to you in the present moment. When you're disassociated, it's as if you watch yourself going through the experience, much like watching a movie. The "you" in the movie may even seem like someone else.

We can all associate and disassociate, but typically, you're prone to one or the other in daily life. For instance, you may see a sad film or someone in pain, and feel immediately distressed, as if it's happening to you. Or you may be the type of person who easily steps back and watches events from a distance. Both skills are helpful. By associating, you can more easily understand where another person is coming from. By disassociating, you're often more able to see the big picture. Both approaches are used in the MER process.

In MER, disassociation is especially important when dealing with trauma or overwhelming negative emotions. Unlike other therapies, clients do *not* have to re-experience a painful event to release its emotions and impact on their life.

In one of my workshops in Las Vegas not long ago, I had just completed a demonstration with a lady who had been physically abused and almost killed by her ex-husband. Another person in the group (who had also volunteered for the demo) was a former teacher who had been in a school shooting right after Columbine. In the middle of doing the release with the entire group, this former teacher went into a full phobic response.

Recognizing what was occurring, I brought her up on stage and asked her if it was okay to release her negative emotions around the experience. I took her to a modified MER process. This modified process (see chapter 9) is most useful for phobic responses because we use a double dissociation to let go of the deeper baggage without inciting the phobic response. (Please note: For phobias as intense as this one, it's important that the practitioner is someone fully trained and experienced in the technique and in dealing with phobias.) After taking her through the release process, she began to cry tears that she said were from relief. She said she still felt for the families who had lost children.

Then she smiled softly, saying, "But I am alive, and I had helped as many children as I could."

On the next break, she came up to me and told me that a weight had been lifted from her, and she was finally free of the negative emotions from that horrible event. She has since attended other events and shared with my groups how empowering it is to be free of the emotions. It was still a tragic event; however, the baggage is now gone.

Retaining the Learnings

As we discussed, the unconscious mind is a highly skilled learner. It takes each experience and wrings out of it any lessons it needs to help you survive. And as I mentioned, sometimes the conclusions it draws from experiences are not accurate or shouldn't be generalized. If toddlers are scratched by a cat, they are wise to be careful around that particular cat. That's a good learning. But as they grow up, if that lesson gets generalized to all cats, and rather than caution they experience terror around cats, that lesson has become inappropriate.

Because root cause events of major negative emotions happen during early childhood, the unconscious mind was still naïve when the lesson was learned. It was brilliant learning for a four-year-old, but not so much for an adult. For example, as a toddler, you may have figured out that you wouldn't get yelled at if you were seen and not heard. Not expressing yourself may have felt safer as a little one, but it certainly limits you as an adult.

Within the MER process, the unconscious is invited to incorporate or find a new learning, one that will serve you better. Your unconscious is able to take the wisdom and knowledge you have as an adult and apply it to the old event to gain a different perspective and a new truth. It is then this new truth that directs your actions and reactions. For some clients, the new learning is understood immediately. And for others, sometimes the learning is preserved at the unconscious level for later use. However it happens is perfect because the new learning replaces the baggage.

Here is a quick example on learnings and why they are so important to the MER process: My daughter Skylar had no fear of the dark when she was a baby. In fact, we had to make sure the room was completely blacked out, or she wouldn't be able to sleep. One day I came back from a training, and she had a night light in her room. The next morning, I asked her why she had a night light when, in fact, she had no fear of the dark.

She responded by saying, "Daddy, I *am* afraid of the dark."

I told her about how when she was a baby, she needed the entire room blacked out, and again I said, "You are not afraid of the dark."

She responded with, "Well, Daddy, I am now."

I couldn't argue with that.

One night, she came into the room and tapped me on the shoulder while I was sleeping. She woke me up because her nightlight had gone out. I decided this was a good time to teach her something. I asked her how she got into the room if it was so dark.

She looked around and said, "Wow, Daddy, I can see in the dark."

I said, "Right, now go back to bed."

The next morning, we had a discussion about the fact that fear of the dark is unnecessary once you learn (these are the learnings) that you can see when you allow your eyes to adjust. That knowledge prevented her fear of the dark from coming back.

It is the learnings that prevent the baggage from ever coming back.

6

Steps in the MER Process

Overview of the Technique

The technique itself follows a very specific protocol to get the best possible result. (To find out how to receive training and certification in Mental and Emotional Release therapy, please go to EmpowermentPartnership.com or my personal site, DrMatt.com). Here is a brief overview of those steps (please read this before going to the section on the exact process):

1. Comprehensive personal history. To begin the process, a Master Practitioner trained in MER asks specific questions to identify the greater problem, the underlying limiting belief or emotion that holds unwanted symptoms in place. For example, issues surrounding career or money might have an overall underlying belief of "I just don't have what it takes" or "I'm broken." To get to this greater problem, we focus on context, not content. In other words, we don't delve into details of early childhood (who said what to whom, etc.), but we look for themes. For instance, a client may report feeling "stupid" in kindergarten, then "stupid" when he played family board games, and "stupid" when he was fired from his first job.

Note to Practitioners: It's critical that the practitioner records the client's statements in *their own words,* without editing or changing the language. The specific way a client states issues is the voice that the unconscious will recognize and respond to.

2. Determine specific outcomes and measures of success. The basic inquiry here is, "How will you know that you have achieved your desired outcome?" For example, a client dealing with career issues might say, "I'd feel comfortable stating my opinions to my boss," or "I'd feel confident taking steps to start my own business."

Note to Practitioners: Outcomes are not goals. Goals are specific results clients want to create that they will work toward. Outcomes let you know that the work you have done was effective. They measure whether the client's issues have been resolved. "I feel confident and clear about steps I must take to build my business" is an outcome. "I make $100,000 this year in my business" is a goal. Also, it's important to make sure outcomes are stated in the positive ("I feel smart and capable" versus "I don't feel dumb anymore") and can be verified by the client in the near future ("I feel comfortable and enjoy being with children" versus "I'll be a great parent twenty years from now").

3. Elicit values. One of the primary principles of NLP is that any changes made must fit in with a client's value system. When your values are in conflict with one another, desired changes are often difficult. For example, if you're someone who strongly values financial security, your desire to become entrepreneurial and take big risks may be at odds with that value. In this part of the process, we unearth those conflicts and then check back at the completion of MER to make sure values have shifted or conflicts have been resolved.

4. Discuss the four requisites to create empowerment and change. A client needs to understand and honor the four requisites for change for the Mental and Emotional Release process to be successful. This type of work is a "do with" process, not a "do to" process. In other words, the practitioner is not set up to "fix" the client. Client and practitioner act as partners to achieve the desired outcomes.

The first requisite is to release negative emotions and limiting beliefs. This is done through the MER process as well as other techniques.

The second requisite is to set positive goals for the future. You need to have a goal or a focus for the future.

Both of these parts of the process are guided by the practitioner, with the client's full participation.

The third requisite is that clients must take action toward their goals and must take action that aligns with their new perspective. This is often automatic. A client who shifts from feeling "unattractive and unlikeable" to "attractive and likeable" will naturally be more open and friendly. However, once clients go back to their old environment, it's possible to slip into old patterns.

For instance, a client of one of my students experienced a substantial shift from "I'm broken and incompetent" to "I feel confident trying new things, and I feel strong and capable." When she returned home, she was surrounded by friends and family who still perceived her as weak and fragile. She noticed that it was easy to slip into the old pattern of allowing others to make decisions for her and tell her what to do. Support and follow-through with a practitioner is critical at this stage.

The fourth requisite is for the client to maintain focus after the MER is complete. Maintaining focus means to understand that everything that happens going forward is an integral, appropriate part of the process. To illustrate, think of getting up from a seat in your living room to go to the far end of your home. To make that journey, typically you'll have to go through doorways, step around chairs or tables, maybe even walk up or down stairs. These apparent obstacles are indications that you're moving forward. If you stayed in your seat, you'd have no obstacles, but you'd also have no movement. Focus means to notice what comes up as you move forward and acknowledge it as part of your process. You want to be aware of your responses to whatever comes up and how they differ from your old reactions.

Note to Practitioners: Typically, this first phase of MER takes one or two hours. Many practitioners choose to do the steps 1 through 4 one day, organize their notes, and then take the client through the rest of the process on another day, in a breakthrough session or in a few sessions. If these first steps are done correctly using specific NLP techniques (chunking up or chunking down, meta language inquiry, etc.), the intake alone will begin to loosen up a client's issues and problems. It's important to advise clients that the intake may stir up the pot, so they should drink plenty of water and get rest, even after this first session.

5. Determine the client's time line. As we discussed, each of us has our own time line. In this step, we help clients recognize how their time line is configured. In the rare incidents when clients' time lines are *not* linear, Master Practitioners can help them modify their time line to make it easier to use for this process. But this must be done carefully and must honor the unconscious mind's particular organizational system.

6. Test-drive floating above the time line. We ask clients to float above their time line, moving into the past and into the future, to get comfortable with the process. Clients find it surprisingly simple to do, even if they claim they are not good at visualization or imagery. One of the important steps during this test-drive is to have the client float high enough above the time line until they are completely disassociated with any events on it. We call this the "bail-out" position. It's like a safe haven and is particularly important to establish for clients who have experienced trauma.

The next steps are considered the intervention phase of MER. Steps 7 through 11 are repeated with each major negative emotion (anger, sadness, fear, hurt, guilt) and any limiting beliefs that have not automatically released after the major negative emotions.

7. Ask permission from the unconscious. As many of us know, issues and negative emotions often have secondary gains or some purpose in the scheme of things. A person who gets very angry at being disrespected may view that anger as a protective mechanism. People who are sad may think their continued grief honors a lost loved one. People with a strong sense of guilt may think their guilt keeps them from doing harm.

So we begin each round of releasing by asking, "Is it okay with your unconscious mind to release this negative emotion [or belief] today, for you to be aware of it consciously?" If the answer is no, it's possible to help clients reframe whatever reason they have for hanging on to that negative emotion or belief. If the unconscious still resists, the client may not be ready for this work or the practitioner may not have established sufficient rapport with the client's unconscious mind.

8. Elicit the root cause. With good rapport established with the unconscious mind, this step becomes as simple as asking the unconscious mind, "What is the root cause of this problem, the first event which, when disconnected, will cause the problem to disappear?" The practitioner then goes through a series of questions to pinpoint the timing of this event. The client's job in this step is to simply say whatever comes up and avoid second-guessing or overanalyzing.

A couple of notes about root cause. Often, this root cause event seems insignificant, not the dramatic incident you might expect. Also, it's not uncommon for clients to never see or know consciously what the event is.

Note to Practitioners: Within the process, if the emotion or belief does *not* release completely, you might need to access an earlier event. (This next diagram represents the three main positions in relationship to an individual's time line.)

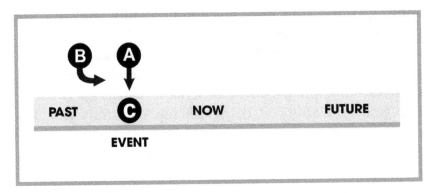

9. Release negative emotions. Using a specific script, the practitioner guides you above your time line into the past to precise positions or perspectives related to that root cause event. You're guided to absorb whatever learnings you need from that event, the learning of which will allow you to release it. Next, you release all of the negative emotions attached to this event. After releasing the negative emotion or belief while floating *above* your time line, you are guided to float down *into* the event itself to verify that the negative emotions and beliefs are indeed gone.

If the negative emotions have not disappeared completely, your practitioner may have you float back further to another position or an earlier root cause event. They may also need to communicate with your unconscious to address resistance or reframe any secondary gains.

Note to Practitioners: For clients who associate easily, use Negative Emotions 1 (explained below). For those who have difficulty accessing their emotions, use Negative Emotions 2. Remember, clients should *not* have to experience strong negative emotions or traumatic events. If they become too associated with an event, have them float higher to a safer location.

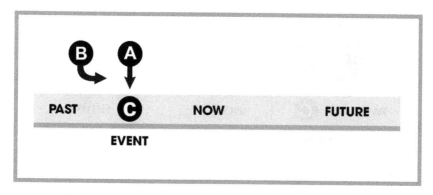

10. Release the emotion or negative belief on all subsequent events. Staying above your time line, you are guided to retain the learnings and release the emotions or limiting beliefs as you float back to the present. This is a deceptively simple process that should only take a few minutes. (If it takes longer, it's possible that the client is floating *into* subsequent events rather than staying above the time line.)

11. Test with past memory and future event. An MER session is only successful if you experience a total release of the emotion or belief being processed. It must be your own internal sense of knowing that the issue is gone completely, not an external perception of the practitioner. If the release does *not* feel complete, either the root cause was not correctly identified or there is a similar (but different) emotion or belief that needs to be addressed.

To test this, your practitioner will simply ask you to recall an event in the past that would have brought up that old emotion or belief to see if it feels different. Next, they will ask you to imagine a future event that might have elicited that old emotion or negative belief and see if what was released shows up. If both are clear, you proceed to the next emotion or belief.

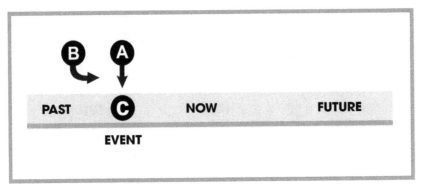

12. Handle outstanding issues. After you've completed the Mental and Emotional Release process with all major negative emotions and limiting beliefs, 99 percent of all your issues in that particular area should have disappeared. But for any that remain, this is the point where a skilled practitioner will clean up those issues using various NLP techniques such as Parts Integration, Chaining Anchors, Prime Concerns, SWISH Pattern, and Like to Dislike.

13. Re-elicit values. The process is the same as Step 3. Most people find that their values have shifted and that they are much more congruent and aligned. If these values do *not* support the changes you made, you will experience internal conflict and have difficulty following through. So your practitioner checks on your values and uses various techniques to help get them aligned (Parts Integration, Values Hierarchy, etc.).

14. Complete the changes. Practitioners use light hypnosis or pendulum work to ensure that the unconscious mind assists and supports the changes you've made. You'll also be guided to travel one, five, and ten years into the future on your time line to see how the changes you've made have evolved. At this stage, you'll also revisit your desired outcomes and verify that your MER session has accomplished them.

15. Set future goals. As one of the requisites for lasting change, your practitioner will help you set meaningful goals for yourself in the future. They use the SMART goal acronym to make sure any goals are formed properly and then install them into your time line using a specific process. (For a comprehensive report on Goal Setting and Goal Getting, email info@nlp.com.)

16. Schedule a follow-up session. Though you may experience immediate results from the MER session, your follow-up session is an important component in ensuring that your changes remain in effect. Changes made during an MER session are significant. And because these changes occur in the unconscious mind, they can initially be confusing or even disorienting. Old patterns and behaviors disappear as new strategies emerge. To help keep you on track, your practitioner will schedule a follow-up session a week or two after your session, assign you specific tasks, and give you additional tools for any issues that arise.

The Script and Process

The process you are about to experience has been improved, revised, and refined since the late 1980s. As you will read in later chapters, we now have hundreds of case studies as well as clinical and academic research to validate the effectiveness of MER.

Personally and professionally, I have wanted to get as much information out to the public as I possibly can, because I believe everybody deserves to be free of their baggage. And as a Doctor of Psychology, I need to balance that with the idea that the most important person in the therapeutic equation is the client. The person who is receiving the release work needs to be cared for and nurtured the most.

Therefore, if you believe that your issue is greater than or deeper than something that can be handled by reading a book, we host live events; professionals who have been trained in MER are ready and willing to assist you. Also, if you believe that you want to learn to help people with their baggage, please realize a book is not sufficient to do any type of deep issue work.

There are many techniques that make up MER. I will be sharing two of them with you here in specific detail. The first one is called Negative Emotions 1. This technique is good for general anger, sadness, fear, hurt, guilt, and any other past-based negative emotion. It is not for trauma, nor do I use it for phobia and other major disorders. There are many other things that you would need to do when working on deeper issues, including a full MER Break Through Session, along with a Detailed Personal History.

The other technique I will share with you is the MER anxiety release, a very simple and easy technique that alleviates and releases anxiety. It is helpful to have released past-based fear when beginning to work with anxiety, and we will discuss that later.

Negative Emotions 1

To be able to release past-based negative emotions, you need to do two processes. First is the root cause elicitation, and second is the release of the negative emotions. Each negative emotion has a gestalt and a root cause, as we previously discussed. So each time you release a specific negative emotion, you elicit the root cause and then go into the actual release work. As I teach at our advanced MER trainings as well as in our introductory event called Empowering Your Life, this two-pronged approach needs to be done every single time you work on an emotion. The following is the root cause elicitation that you would use with each negative emotion that is rooted in the past.

Discovering Root Cause Script

Note: This section is done before the client is above the time line. It increases unconscious trust and cooperation.

1. Ask, Is it all right with your unconscious mind for you to release this emotion [or limiting belief] today and for you to be aware of it consciously?
2. Find the first event: What is the root cause of this problem, the first event which, when disconnected, will cause the problem to disappear?

If you were to know, was it before, during, or after your birth?

BEFORE: "In the womb or before?"

WOMB: "What month?"

BEFORE: "Was it a past life or passed down to you genealogically?"

PAST LIFE: "How many lifetimes ago?"

GENEALOGICAL: "How many generations ago?"

AFTER: "If you were to know, what age were you?"

If client says, "I don't know what the root cause is," then respond with, "I know you don't, but if you did, take whatever comes up; trust your unconscious mind."

If client says both genealogical and past life, work with the earlier one first, then the later.

Ratify the change: Verify conscious acknowledgment of shift. When a major physiological shift occurs in the client, be sure to mention it: "That was a big one, wasn't it?"

When you are eliciting the root cause for a limiting belief, note if the client is at cause. If not, then ask for the limiting decision that caused the limiting belief in question.

Next is the actual release work. So once you have the root cause of the specific negative emotion, you now have the deepest aspect of the gestalt. Once you have that, you focus on the release. Here is the script that you would go through in order to release the entire gestalt:

Negative Emotions 1 Script
Procedure

1. "Just float up above your time line and over the past to position A, facing the past, and directly up above the event so you are looking down on the event. Let me know when you are there."

2. "Ask your unconscious mind what it needs to learn from the event, the learning of which will allow you to let go of the emotions easily and effortlessly. Your unconscious mind can preserve the learnings so that if you need them in the future, they'll be there. Just tell your unconscious mind to preserve the learnings."

3. "Now, float to position B so you are above the event and before the event, and you are looking toward now. (Make sure you are well before any of the chain of events that led to that event.) And ask yourself, 'Now, where are the emotions?'"

4. "Float down inside the event to position C, looking through your own eyes, and check on the emotions. Are they there? Or have they disappeared! Now!! Good, go back to position B."

5. "Now, come back to now above your time line only as quickly as you can let go of all the [name the emotion] on the events, all the way back to now; assume position B with each subsequent event,

preserve the learnings, and let go of the [name the emotion] all the way back to now. [When client is done] Float down into now and come back into the room." [Break state]

6. Test: [Client back at now.] "Can you remember any event in the past where you used to be able to feel that old emotion? Go back and notice if you can feel it, or you may find that you cannot. Good; come back to now."

7. Future pace: [Client back at now.] "I want you to go out into the future to an unspecified time in the future which, if it had happened in the past, you would have felt inappropriate or unwarranted [name the emotion], and notice if you can find that old emotion, or you may find that you cannot. Okay? Good; come back to now."

If while you are in position B, the emotion does not release, there are a few things that you can do. Again, I must caution you that if you get stuck, then I would highly recommend that you seek out assistance from a trained professional. If at any point during this process, you feel that this maybe more than a book could handle, you might want to see a trained professional for one-on-one release work.

Three Things to Check at Position B
1. Make sure client is in position B.
   (Indicator: Client is really feeling the emotions.)

Tell client:

"Get up higher, and float farther back."

"Get high enough and far enough back until the emotion disappears."

2. Be sure client is before the first event. (Indicator: 90 percent of the emotions release.)

    Ask client:

    "Are you before the first event?"

    "Is there an event earlier than this one? Go back before the first one."

3. Must be totally agreeable to let go of the emotion. (Indicator: Client says, "The emotions are not releasing.")

    Ask client:

    "What is there to learn from this event? If you learn this, won't it be better than having the old emotions? How can you get the same benefit that the emotions provided when you let them go?"

MER Anxiety Model

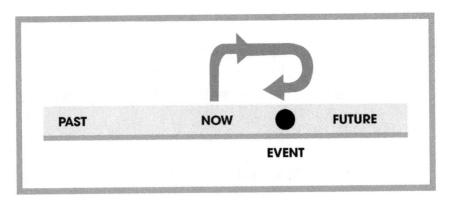

In a recent interview for the World Summit at Hay House Publishing, I took the group through a guided experience of releasing anxiety. It is actually not that difficult to do. Anxiety is a warning from the unconscious mind to focus on the positive. In other words, people with anxiety install negative events in their future. There is no root cause elicitation, nor is there any gestalt. It is a single event and can be handled very quickly. The key is in making sure that you see, hear, and feel the event ending positively. Here is the script:

MER Anxiety Script
Procedure: (Make sure you are working on a specific event.)

1. "What are you anxious about? What specifically?"
2. "Good, just float up above the time line."
3. "And float out above the future to fifteen minutes after the successful completion of the event about which you thought you were anxious. Tell me when you're there."
4. "Good. Turn and look toward now, along the time line."
5. "Now, where's the anxiety?"
   (If client says, "It's gone," go to 6.)

   (If client says, "It's still there," then ask, "Are you imagining it completing successfully?" If "No," then talk about successful completion for the event and then to go 3.)

6. "Come back to now."
7. If desired, test by having clients think about what used to make them anxious and notice that there is no anxiety.
8. If you are eliminating all anxiety, then go to 1 using a new event.

It is significantly easier to release anxiety if you have also released past-based fear. So I highly recommend doing that first. Furthermore, the key is in making sure that you see, hear, and feel the event ending in a positive way.

We all know bad things happen. I have this funny slogan on the back of Empowerment Partnership T-shirts: "SHIfT happens."

One of my clients asked me, "But Dr. Matt, what if the bad things still happen?"

My response was, "Well, then we deal with it. And will putting positive things in the future increase the likelihood for positive experiences?" Yes! "Will putting negative things in the future increase the likelihood of you experiencing negative results?" Yes!

So simply put, we should put positive things out there.

Caution Regarding Working with Yourself and Especially Others

I cannot emphasize enough the importance of working with someone else. I would never extract a tooth, drill a cavity, conduct open heart surgery, or mend a broken leg on myself or a loved one, unless I was specifically trained to do so. (I think you get my point.)

In other words, as a Doctor of Psychology, I've had a significant amount of training to be able to work with other individuals. My students who have been trained in MER, on average, have taken more than three hundred hours of training to be able to learn how to do MER with other people.

I do believe that some people can read a book and experience a significant amount of release work. But if your issue is deeper, or you believe it would be very helpful to have someone else assisting you, please contact our office so that we can provide you with resources. We have audio recordings of live trainings and individuals who can help you get in touch with and release the deeper level baggage.

Overall, that is the simpler aspects of the MER process.

In the next chapters, I'll discuss how this seemingly simple technique works with various disorders and life issues. I've devoted complete chapters to depression, PTSD, and phobia: three major disorders that other therapies have had limited success in treating. Next, I'll share case studies about a variety of other disorders, not with the intent of covering every ailment where MER can be effective but to show you its breadth. Then in chapter 10, I'll share case studies of clients who had no obvious disorder yet felt blocked in their growth or success in life.

7

Mental and Emotional Release and Depression

Imagine having a great day where the skies are blue and sun is shining so brightly. You're cruising through the life without a care in the world, and all of a sudden, a few clouds roll in. Then the clouds get darker. The wind picks up a little, and it begins to get cold. Suddenly, it's raining and dark and dreary. Those blue skies are just a distant memory. Tris Thorp, who wrote chapter 4, describes depression like that as a sudden cloudy day.

One of my clients and long-term students, Barbara, had been on antidepressants for twenty years. While I support using medication to help stabilize an existing problem, my degree in Integrative Health Psychology has taught me that the deeper issue or underlying baggage must also be resolved. Barbara had sadness for as long as she could remember. From a health psychology perspective, depression is overwhelming sadness. Her sadness came from early childhood loss: the loss of her mother and the loss of her father. As a young adult, she lost another loved one and never fully released or coped with the loss. After eight hours of NLP and MER, and nine months of slowing weaning her body off the medications (under the supervision of her MD), Barbara became medication-free and has stayed that way for eight years now. It's as if the storm that rolled in suddenly broke. A little bit of blue sky was able to peek through, and the sun is now shining brightly again.

Depression Defined

Depression is now more common than AIDS, cancer, and diabetes combined; nearly four hundred thousand people attempt suicide in the United States every year.

Of course, there are different levels of depression. It can range from a mild, temporary sense of sadness to a severe, persistent feeling of hopelessness or despondency. When doctors use the term "clinical depression," they are referring to the more severe, lasting form of depression, which is also called major depression or major depressive disorder. A large segment of the population will suffer from chronic depressive symptoms over the course of their lifespan.

Clinical depression has become the leading cause of disability in the United States for people who are fifteen to forty-four years old. In any given year, major depressive disorder affects approximately 14.8 million American adults, or about 6.7 percent of the US population age eighteen and older. It can affect people of any age and either sex, including children, but the median age in the United States is thirty-two.[12]

In all types of depression, no matter what the source or cause, there are several classic signs and symptoms that therapists recognize. These include sadness or a sense of emptiness, feelings of hopelessness or helplessness, suicidal thoughts, irritability, poor concentration, loss or gain of body weight (that is more than 5 percent and not related to intentional dieting or other health issues), poor self-esteem, the inability to experience pleasure, and listlessness and lethargy. According to the American Psychiatric Association, between 3 and 17 percent of us will experience at least one major depressive episode in

---

[12] http://archpsyc.jamanetwork.com/article.
aspx?articleid=208678

our lifetime that lasts two weeks or more and includes at least five of those classic symptoms. Often, this is caused by a traumatic event such as the death of a loved one or loss of a job.

Along with the classic symptoms, it's interesting to note men and women can experience depression slightly differently. Men are more likely to report fatigue and other physical ailments (stomachache, headache, back pain, constipation, diarrhea, etc.) and complain about sleep problems (either not being able to sleep or sleeping too much). Often, men find themselves feeling constantly angry or hostile rather than sad. They often describe themselves as being "stressed" rather than depressed, and they may complain of loss of sexual desire and erectile dysfunction.[13]

Depression caused by a medical condition (such as a thyroid problem) or by substance abuse is not considered clinical depression. And the period of natural depression that occurs after a serious loss (such as death of a loved one, loss of a job or income, etc.) is only considered major depression if it doesn't resolve itself within a few months. When you suffer from true clinical depression, you tend to have difficulty in several areas of life. You may not be able to communicate or relate well with those around you. You may isolate yourself and not engage in your normal activities. You may spend half the day weeping and the other half sleeping or have volatile bursts of anger for no apparent reason. You might stop eating and lose all interest in taking care of yourself physically, and you may be unable to function at work or in school.

How Depression Is Typically Treated

Since the 1970s, modern psychiatry has primarily viewed clinical depression as a chemical imbalance. Scientists identified that monoamines, which are mood-related chemicals such as serotonin, norepinephrine, and

---

[13] http://www.webmd.com/depression/depression-men

dopamine, are low in the brain during major depressive episodes. Their conclusion was that the solution is to increase these missing chemicals via medication to reduce symptoms of depression.

But even though antidepressants are the treatment of choice today, research doesn't support it. In 1975, Stanford psychiatrist David Burns and his team administered high doses of L-tryptophan to increase serotonin levels in clinically depressed veterans. The massive doses *should* have relieved the depression, but they didn't.[14] In 2002, psychologist Irving Kirsch, now of Harvard, ran a meta-analysis of data from drug trials for antidepressants submitted to the Food and Drug Administration (FDA) between 1987 and 1999 (published and unpublished). The analysis showed that the difference between results of the antidepressant drugs and the placebos was not clinically significant.

Despite these findings, the widely accepted and most common approach to treating clinical depression is to combine psychopharmacological treatment (antidepressants) with some form of psychological therapy.

How MER Works with Depression

In MER, we view depression as a series of thought patterns and habitual emotional responses that combine to create a depressive state, which then becomes your baseline state. It's a "process" you do rather than a "thing" you have. For example, you consistently think thoughts like *Life sucks* or *I'll never get out of this hole*. You "decide" to feel sad or angry about certain circumstances. Your body reacts with pain or fear. You actually do all these things *unconsciously*, and working with the unconscious, you have the power to do them differently (though people who experience major depression certainly don't feel as if they have that power).

Typically in MER, we focus on a certain area of life:

---

14   *Stanford Alumni Magazine*, September 2013.

career, relationships, health, personal growth, or spiritual development. Clients may be able to pinpoint when their depression began (though its root will typically be prior to that conscious event) and which area it is most attached to, or they may not. Because depression tends to spread into all areas of life, it may not be immediately obvious. But working with major negative emotions in any area will loosen the depression and clear away enough to determine a root cause. In other words, a client's depression may have its root cause in the area of relationships. If you run through the MER process with a focus on career, the depression will loosen and lead you to the next appropriate steps toward the root cause of the depression.

Depression has physical and chemical components and patterns. So though you may experience immediate relief from the depression with an MER session, follow-up is particularly important. For example, the following is from a recent article from the National Institute of Mental Health (NIMH):

> Bodily aches and pains are a common symptom of depression. Studies show that people with more severe depression feel more intense pain. According to recent research, people with depression have higher than normal levels of proteins called cytokines. Cytokines send messages to cells that affect how the immune system responds to infection and disease, including the strength and length of the response. In this way, cytokines can trigger pain by promoting inflammation, which is the body's response to infection or injury. Inflammation helps protect the body by destroying, removing, or isolating the infected or injured area. In addition to pain, signs of

inflammation include swelling, redness, heat, and sometimes loss of function.[15]

A specific disease that often occurs with depression is fibromyalgia.[16] Fibromyalgia causes chronic fatigue, widespread muscle pain, and various places on the body that are tender and painful, even when touched with light pressure.[17]

Major depression is invasive, affecting the client physically, emotionally, and mentally on many levels. Because of this, I recommend that clients with major depression work with MER practitioners who have additional therapeutic training and commit to a longer period of follow-up to ensure the depression is fully released.

It's particularly important to get the unconscious mind's agreement that it is willing to release the depression. Depression can become a way of life and create a strong identity. As uncomfortable as it is, depression can be feel like a safe place to hide from the ups and downs of life. Especially if they have experienced depression for a long time, clients may fear the unknown of living with energy and optimism. A skilled practitioner will unearth any secondary gains from the depression and address them first before proceeding with the intervention phase of MER.

If a client has been diagnosed as clinically depressed and is receiving treatment, it's critical that the practitioner coordinate efforts with that client's physician or therapist. After MER, many clients find that they can reduce or

---

[15] http://www.ninds.nih.gov/disorders/chronic_pain/detail_chronic_pain.htm#140523084.

[16] Staud, R. "Biology and therapy of fibromyalgia: pain in fibromyalgia syndrome." *Arthritis Research & Therapy* 8(3):208, 2006.

[17] http://www.niams.nih.gov/Health_Info/Fibromyalgia/default.asp

eliminate their medications, but this should be done carefully and with supervision.

Throughout this book, I've given examples showing how MER can be a rapid and effective tool for depressive symptoms. But the following story from one of my students (who is a skilled psychotherapist) illustrates how it can also be used for longer term therapy in clients who are profoundly depressed. When clients are profoundly depressed, they often lack the basic motivation to do anything at all toward their own well-being:

Jessica, a young woman in her mid-twenties, came to my student complaining of "paralyzing depression." Earlier in her twenties, Jessica had been hooked on methamphetamine for about two years. Through an intervention by her family, she went into rehab and successfully kicked her addiction. Though she credited rehab for saving her life, Jessica had felt depressed ever since.

Just prior to coming to my student for help, Jessica had been dating a young man who lived in her apartment building for several months. She thought the relationship was going well until she discovered that her boyfriend, Sean, was also dating another woman. Jessica was very hurt, even though she and Sean had never defined their relationship as exclusive. Sean ultimately chose the other woman and eventually married her.

Jessica was devastated. She told my student that she was barely functioning, and while not suicidal per se, she felt that her life was not worth living. She described feeling hopeless and helpless, as well as having difficulty sleeping. She rapidly gained a significant amount of weight and said that, apart from going to work, she did nothing but eat and watch TV, often not leaving her house for days at a time.

My student describes Jessica as a particularly difficult and resistant client. She did not follow through on any of the homework my student assigned or listen to any of the CDs he offered her to relieve her symptoms. She was reluctant to try MER but agreed to experience it after several sessions. As my student explained it, "Treatment was slow and methodical, as Jessica's depression was so profound, she would do little or nothing between sessions. Her treatment continued for two years with multiple MER sessions spaced out over several months."

After two years of regular treatment, Jessica was able to get off of all antidepressants. She lost her excess weight, was promoted at work, and started a positive relationship with a new boyfriend. She forgave her prior boyfriend and recently helped him celebrate the birth of his new baby boy. She still doesn't describe herself as "joyful and extremely happy," but Jessica is now motivated to take care of herself and "create a life worth living."

8

Mental and Emotional Release and Post-Traumatic Stress Disorder

Twenty-eight-year-old Warren was an active-duty staff sergeant in the Air Force, working in logistics. He had struggled with anger through much of his life, but when he got so angry with a subordinate that he choked him and nearly killed him, Warren called for an appointment with my student, Dr. Patrick Scott, who said, "He talked about feeling stressed. His wife was pregnant with their first child, and Warren was nervous about becoming a father." Along with stress, Warren talked about difficulty sleeping, bouts of sadness, and frequent feelings of anxiety.

As Warren released negative emotions using the MER technique, other issues began to surface. Dr. Scott said, "Warren talked about a couple of combat experiences while he was deployed in Afghanistan. In one, he was in a motorcade when an IED [improvised explosive device] exploded beneath the Humvee in front of him, killing four of his close friends. Warren had avoided thinking about it for nearly a year. But when it came up, he felt racked with guilt." Dr. Scott guided Warren through the MER Phobia Model (see chapter 9) to deal with that particular event.

"What happened next was interesting," Dr. Scott said. "The guilt was released, but when Warren returned the next week, he said he felt angrier than ever. It was like peeling

back an onion." As they explored the root cause of this anger, Warren recalled an incident when he was four years old: "His father found Warren playing with matches. He grabbed the child by the back of the neck and threw him across the room. Warren remembers slamming into a bookcase and falling to the ground as his father continued to yell at him." Again using the MER Phobia Model, Warren was able to release the anger and fear of that event. "Within two weeks, Warren reported that his anger issues and other symptoms were completely gone."

PTSD Defined

Post-traumatic stress disorder (PTSD) is a condition that's triggered by a terrifying or traumatic event. By definition, PTSD always follows a traumatic event that makes the person feel intense fear or helplessness. Often the symptoms develop shortly after the event, but it may take years. The duration for symptoms must be for at least one month to be diagnosed as PTSD.

A National Vietnam Veterans' Readjustment Study initially found that 15 percent of Vietnam veterans had PTSD at the time of the study (1980), and 30 percent had PTSD at some point in their life. But a 2003 review found that "a large majority of Vietnam Veterans struggled with chronic PTSD symptoms, with 4 out of 5 reporting recent symptoms when interviewed 20-25 years after Vietnam."[18] According to statistics from the Department of Veterans Affairs, 476,515 veterans with primary or secondary diagnosis of PTSD received treatment at VA medical centers and clinics in 2011.[19]

Post-traumatic stress disorder is not confined to combat personnel. Two years after the 9/11 attacks, *New York Magazine* reported that "probably half the city's firefighters

---

[18] http://www.ptsd.va.gov/professional/research-bio/research/vietnam-vets-study.asp

[19] http://www.va.gov/opa/issues/PTSD.asp

have gone into therapy and 6,100 uniformed people have received counseling through the department."[20] In a study conducted by the University of Michigan after Hurricane Katrina, researchers interviewed 810 people in Mississippi's twenty-three southernmost counties and found that more than 22 percent showed symptoms of PTSD.[21] Post-traumatic stress disorder can be caused by acts of violence, sexual abuse, kidnapping, or rape, along with cataclysmic weather conditions like tornadoes or hurricanes, or natural disasters like earthquakes. It can also occur from severe physical pain and injury, traumatic death of a loved one, or any other experience that is shocking or seems to threaten survival.

Technically, PTSD is classified as an anxiety disorder. Its symptoms are generally grouped into three types:

1. Intrusive memories: flashbacks or reliving the traumatic event for minutes or even days at a time, or upsetting dreams about the event
2. Avoidance or numbing: resisting thinking or talking about the event, feeling emotionally numb, avoiding activities that were once enjoyable, sense of hopelessness about the future, memory difficulties, trouble concentrating, difficulty maintaining close relationships
3. Hyper-arousal: increased anxiety or extreme emotional reactions, chronic irritability or anger, overwhelming guilt or shame, self-destructive behavior (like drinking too much), problems with sleeping, being easily startled or frightened, hearing or seeing things that aren't there, severe anxiety

---

[20] http://nymag.com/nymetro/news/sept11/2003/n_9189/index1.html
[21] http://www.ur.umich.edu/0708/Apr28_08/11.php

As Dr. Bessel van der Kolk, a clinical psychiatrist who studied PTSD for over three decades, explains it, "Ordinarily, memories of particular events are remembered as stories that change and deteriorate over time and that do not evoke intense emotions and sensations. In contrast, in PTSD the past is relived with an immediate sensory and emotional intensity that makes victims feel as if the event were occurring all over again."[22]

Researchers at the Department of Veterans Affairs estimate that more than half of us will experience at least one traumatizing event over our lifetimes. Statistically, men are more likely to experience a traumatic event, but women are more likely to experience the high-impact types of traumatic events that can lead to PTSD, such as domestic violence or sexual assault. Only a minority of people who face trauma develop PTSD, but they are more likely to be women. According to the National Collaborating Center for Mental Health, the average risk of developing PTSD after trauma is about 8 percent for men (though the average for men who have been in combat is closer to 20 percent), and just over 20 percent for women.[23]

Alisha was eighteen years old when she experienced the trauma of rape. Two armed men broke into her family's home. They tied up Alisha's parents and brutally raped her and her three sisters.

The entire family was traumatized, but Alisha seemed to suffer the most. She had practically stopped eating and was afraid to leave the house. She could not stand to be touched, even by her mother, and she frequently woke up in the middle of the night screaming.

Though violent crime rates in Kingston, Jamaica (where Alisha lives), have fallen over the past few years, a student of mine who lives there, Dr. Rose Johnson, still sees a

---

[22] http://cism.cap.gov/files/articles/PTSD%20&%20Memory%20 -%20BA%20van%20der%20Kolk%20MD.pdf

[23] http://www.ncbi.nlm.nih.gov/books/NBK56506/

significant number of victims of such crimes. In a single session with Alisha, Dr. Rose used MER to release the major negative emotions and followed up with the MER Phobia Model. At the end of this session, the memory of the incident was not erased, but Alisha felt completely neutral about it. Her symptoms disappeared, and she was able to fully engage in life again.

Many of us go through traumatic events and have difficulty adjusting or coping for a short time afterwards. We can have symptoms similar to PTSD, like difficulty sleeping, being easily startled, or irritability. With time, though, most of us begin to feel better. We somehow integrate or accept whatever happened and move on with our lives. But people with PTSD can't do this. The traumatic reaction stays the same (or even gets worse) and can completely disrupt their life. Post-traumatic stress disorder symptoms typically begin within three months of the traumatic event, though in some cases, PTSD symptoms may not show up until years later.

PTSD symptoms can come and go. They might be dormant until life gets stressful in general or until you run into reminders of the traumatic experience. A car backfiring might trigger memories of combat experiences, or you may see a TV news report about a rape and feel overcome by memories of your own assault. People with PTSD might experience unwarranted fear or anxiety, a lack of focus, or sadness. They might have problems sleeping for no apparent reason, unexplainable lack of appetite, or crying spells that catch them off-guard.

How PTSD Is Typically Treated

Though a variety of medications are used to manage the symptoms of PTSD, there is no clear drug treatment for PTSD itself. The NIMH simply states that PTSD can be treated "with psychotherapy ('talk' therapy), medications, or a combination of the two." Much of the research on post-traumatic stress disorder is focused on structures of the brain (i.e., the amygdala and prefrontal cortex) and chemicals in the brain (e.g., stathmin, a protein needed to form fear memories, and gastrin-releasing peptide, which appears to control the fear response). The National Institute of Mental Health is currently studying how the brain responds to different forms of cognitive behavioral therapy (CBT) compared to Zoloft, one of the two drugs recommended and approved by the Food and Drug Administration for treating PTSD.

Paulette, a dynamic independent contractor who consulted with high-powered executives in the banking industry, was a student in one of my practitioners' training seminars. I happened to choose her as a subject for the MER demonstration during that training. Honestly, she only shared a little about her story before we did the technique and released her trauma. But I'll share the details I've learned since to give you an idea of what we were dealing with:

Five years before coming to the practitioners' training, Paulette had suffered a brain hemorrhage from a traumatic brain injury. The surgeons working to save her life gave her only a 5 percent chance of living, and if she did live, they expected she had less than a 2 percent chance that she would have any functioning of her brain at all. She flat-lined three times over a forty-eight-hour period and underwent a death experience. "I was given the choice to come back from the other side," she said, "and I did so."

For the next five years, Paulette wrestled with massive panic attacks: "The trauma wasn't about the death experience. That was fine and even beautiful. The trauma was all the invasive medical procedures that were done to me save my life and the excruciating pain of coming back to life."

Despite doctors' predictions, Paulette was able to recover physically from the ordeal, and she returned to work. But she felt like her emotions were heightened and out of her control. Incidents that seemed to have no relevance to her injury would trigger flashbacks. At least three times a month, she had nightmares and woke up screaming, drenched in sweat. "The panic seemed to get worse every time I stepped into a conference room," she said, "the place where my hemorrhage had burst. I'm a fight girl, not a flight girl. But it got to the point where I couldn't walk into a conference room without taking drugs." She took daily doses of Xanax just to make it through the day.

Like many PTSD sufferers, Paulette couldn't focus and felt like she couldn't contribute as much as she had previously. She started to doubt her abilities and sought consulting projects of increasingly lower responsibility. "My brain just couldn't handle the complexity of thought required for an executive level position," she said. "I know my clients were losing confidence in me as well."

Paulette tried to accept her new limitations, but she was distressed and unhappy: "I was so tired of fighting with willpower alone. I am one spunky and determined chick, but I was spiritually, mentally, emotionally, and physically bankrupt. I began to wish that I'd never come back from the other side."

After several years of struggle, Paulette heard about our practitioners' training and decided to give it a try: "I had made up my mind that if I couldn't get relief from this seminar, I would use the Xanax [forty-six pills] and Flexeril [ninety pills] I had saved to overdose." Paulette had systematically distanced her family and friends so her death wouldn't be such an emotional shock, and she had even made arrangements for her dog.

During the training, when she talked with me about her PTSD, Paulette didn't mention her alternate strategy, and I chose her as my subject to demonstrate MER. Using an abbreviated version of the process, I guided Paulette to release the root cause of her PTSD. It took about fifteen minutes, and she felt instant relief. But it's what she's reported in the months since then that is most striking:

"*Since that day, I haven't taken either Xanax or Flexeril, and I flushed the extra supply I had; no more alternative strategy! I wake up happy, and I actually want to be alive.*

"I remember driving to the office the week right after the training. I was thinking, That had to have been a crock. It was way too easy. It only took fifteen minutes. I've been suffering for five years. How can it work that fast? That dude is smoking crack if he thinks MER fixed me permanently. *But the closer I got to the office, I noticed there was no racing heart, no sweating, no dry mouth, no nausea. I walked into the conference room, sat down, and after thirty minutes, I realized that it was the first time in five years that I hadn't had to excuse myself to go take a Xanax.*

"*When I came to the training, I was in financial difficulty. In a very short time after, I walked into a consulting role with a multimillion-dollar upside. After only ninety days, my life is remarkably different.*"

9

Mental and Emotional Release and Phobia

Phillip was a postgraduate student in anesthesiology. He was motivated and hard-working and completed his studies with excellent grades. But when it came to the final exam, he completely panicked and flunked the final exam, twice. With only one more chance to take the exam and proceed to the next level in his chosen career, Phillip desperately sought out one of my students, Dr. Rose Johnson, to help him.

"He came in saying that maybe he was just too 'dumb' to pass the test," Dr. Rose said. "I ran diagnostics on him and discovered that he actually had superior intelligence, but he was dyslexic, something no one had pinpointed through his entire schooling. The fear and anxiety he had developed around testing was so severe that he broke into a cold sweat even talking about it."

Dr. Rose guided Phillip through the MER, first releasing the five major negative emotions. "As soon as we released fear, his phobia about testing disappeared. Phillip not only passed the exam with flying colors, but now that he knows he has dyslexia, he's found ways to make his studies much easier. He no longer says that he's 'dumb' but tells me that his brain works faster than his hands."

Phobia Defined

The National Institute of Mental Health estimates that about 5 to 12 percent of Americans have phobias. Specific phobias affect an estimated 6.3 million adult Americans.[24] A phobia is an extreme and unreasonable fear of something. It can be fear of things, like mice or clowns or Friday the thirteenth. It can also be fear of certain situations, like driving across a bridge, going to a restaurant, or riding in an elevator. Even though the object or situation doesn't seem particularly dangerous to most of us, people with a phobia about it can feel as though their very life is being threatened. They might feel their heart racing and break out in a sweat. Breathing becomes difficult, and they feel overwhelmed with panic and the desire to flee. Even thinking or talking the object of their phobia can make them extremely anxious.

We've all experienced brief anxiety or fear about things that are not really life-threatening. For instance, you may feel extremely nervous before giving a speech, interviewing for a job, or taking a test. But a phobia is like anxiety on steroids. It's long-lasting, and the physical and psychological reactions it causes are so intense that they affect your ability to function normally. You'll do everything possible to avoid the object of your phobia. And even though you may be conscious of the fact that your fears are irrational (or at least exaggerated), you feel powerless to control them and unable to calm yourself down.

How Phobia Is Typically Treated Today

Most therapists rely on behavioral techniques, although some prescribe drugs to assist treatment. Antidepressants like Celexa, Paxil, Prozac, Lexapro, and Zoloft are used for social phobias, and beta-blockers (mostly propranolol) are used to relieve physical symptoms of anxiety by blocking

---

[24] http://www.webmd.com/anxiety-panic/specific-phobias?page=2

adrenaline that drives the body's response to stress. Sedative-hypnotic drugs (for example, Xanax or Valium) may also be prescribed on the short term.

The following behavioral therapies are commonly used:

Desensitization: This therapy involves gradual, repeated exposure to the cause of the phobia. For example, for people terrified of elevators, they would begin by simply thinking about getting into an elevator. Next, they might look at pictures of elevators. Once viewing a picture of an elevator is relatively comfortable, they would stand near an actual elevator. From standing near an elevator, they would progress to stepping into one. Next, they might ride up one floor, then ride several floors, and finally ride in a crowded elevator. The process could take several months.

Cognitive behavioral therapy: To deal with phobia, CBT usually combines exposure with other techniques to consciously view and cope with the feared object or situation differently. The objective is to consciously master and control your thoughts and feelings about the thing you fear.

Flooding: This technique requires clients to face their fear head-on, and it can be quite traumatic. The theory is that this direct exposure will demonstrate the irrationality of the fear. So under controlled conditions, clients are exposed to what they fear most; using guided relaxation techniques, they attempt to replace their fear with relaxation.

In my opinion, the main problem with these therapies is that they primarily work with the conscious mind. The unconscious mind might be persuaded along the way to give up its fear, or it may not. Additionally, most of them require clients to experience their fear either in small doses over time (desensitization) or in extreme doses (flooding). The fear of phobia is so strong that it can be debilitating, making it almost impossible for some people to even attempt such therapies.

How MER Works with Phobias

In my experience, phobias are typically caused by either a single traumatic event or a series of small events. (An event itself may not even appear to be significant, but the person experiences it as painful or distressing, and the unconscious mind records that event as threatening.)

In one case, a student of mine had a severe phobia of snakes. She had first seen a snake as a little girl and was a bit frightened. A few years later, she was swimming in a river and felt a snake brush up against her leg, and she was more frightened. Sometimes when her father mowed their lawn, he would run over a snake and mangle it, which really disturbed her. Then one day, her brother tossed a snake at her, and that was it. Phobia in place.

Another student had an extreme fear of the weather (definitely a phobia that makes it difficult to function). In her case, she had one traumatic incident that caused it: She had been hit by lightning.

Phobias can also be caused by cultural or familial conditioning. For example, if a parent is fearful of the dentist, that fear can be passed on to his children. The child's unconscious mind picks up that "Dad is anxious about dentists; therefore, something is really bad there." Some researchers believe that certain phobias may even have a genetic component. They theorize that phobias like fear of snakes, insects, or small, dark places could be remnants of the survival instinct of our prehistoric ancestors.

People with a phobia may or may not consciously know its cause, but their unconscious mind has that root cause stored away in its files. When clients do not consciously know the cause of their phobia, or when they identify a series of relatively minor events, we use the MER process to release the primary negative emotions of anger, sadness, fear, hurt, and guilt, as outlined in chapters 5 and 6. The phobia will often disappear using this process alone, as in the example of Phillip at the beginning of this chapter.

But even if it doesn't, releasing negative emotions first ensures that surrounding issues will be uprooted. So to be thorough, practitioners routinely include the release of the primary negative emotions in the process of working with phobias. However, when I'm demonstrating release of phobias in my trainings or if time does not permit including release of all negative emotions in a therapeutic setting, the MER Phobia Model alone is highly effective, as in Nita's story:

In one of my advanced trainings where I teach practitioners how to demonstrate NLP techniques, the students requested a demonstration of the MER Phobia Model. Nita, one of my Master Practitioners, volunteered. Nita, an attractive, confident woman in her thirties, had an intense fear of fish. For decades, she had not been able to go near rivers, streams, lakes, or oceans. She even avoided going to restaurants that had fish on the menu. As Nita described her phobia, the blood drained from her face, sweat appeared on her brow, and she clenched her hands until her knuckles were white.

As we talked about her phobia, Nita remembered an incident as a child. She was on a ferry with her family, and they were feeding the fish. Somehow, the wooden platform she was standing on broke, and she plunged into the water, where she felt thousands of fish nibbling on her.

As we ran the MER Phobia Model, the shift in Nita's physiology was noticeable. Her breathing calmed, and color came back to her face. When the process was complete, she said, "That was so silly. It's just dumb fish!" I asked her if we could test to see if her phobia was indeed gone. Earlier, we had requested the kitchen to bring us some fish, and they brought in a huge dead fish (head, tail, and all) on a large platter. Nita looked at it and asked if she could touch it. She petted the fish and had no reaction to it at all.

Over the years, I've run into Nita and checked on her progress with that old phobia. Finally, she said to me, "Quit asking! It's gone." She went on to become a scuba diver and instructor, and she specializes in helping people with fears of diving.

MER Phobia Model

The MER Phobia Model begins similarly to the MER technique to release primary negative emotions. The root cause or traumatic event is elicited, and clients float above their time line to a place that is above the incident. After they have observed the event and retained the learnings, they are instructed to float to a place that is *before* the event. From here, they create a "movie screen" and see themselves in a theater, watching the screen, and then float up into the projection booth to run a movie of the incident, keeping their attention focused on watching themselves in the audience, watching the event on the screen. This setup ensures that clients are doubly disassociated from the event so they do not have to experience the fear and panic of their phobia.

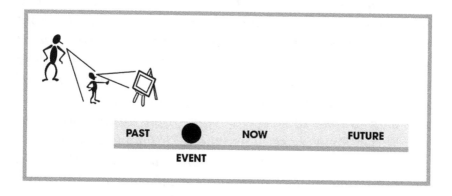

Clients are then guided to run the movie of the root cause event in black-and-white, from start to finish. At the end of the movie, they freeze the frame. Next, they step *into* the movie (become associated) and play it backward in color. When the movie is back to its beginning, they are guided to float back to the projection booth, where they run the movie forward in black-and-white as they watch themselves in the audience watching the movie, stepping into the movie and running it backwards in color. This process is repeated until the fear completely disappears (usually eight to ten times on average).

As simple as it seems, the MER Phobia Model is surprisingly powerful. We have used it successfully not only with severe phobias but also with PTSD. Prior to doing this MER Phobia Model, we make sure clients establish a resource anchor, which acts as a trigger that allows them to instantly feel confident, powerful, and safe. We also make sure that clients are able to float high enough above their time line to the bailout position (discussed in chapter 5) in case they inadvertently associate to the event and experience intense fear.

The stories below illustrate how quickly and completely this technique works:

My student Dr. Rose lives in Jamaica, where phobic reactions to lizards are relatively common. One day, a young woman named Natalie came in to see her, saying, "The more I read about people's fear of croaking lizards, the more terrified I've become, to the point where they have invaded my dreams." Even talking about lizards caused Natalie's hands to shake and her heart beat faster. Her fear had progressed to the point where she avoided darkened rooms and was unable to sleep at night. After talking briefly to Natalie, Dr. Rose chose to use the MER Phobia Model.

When asked, Natalie remembered an incident that was the root cause of her phobia: "As children, one day, my cousins and I sat on a huge rock in the country and stoned a green lizard to death. By the time it died, it had turned black, and we buried it under a pear tree. A few days later, we dug it up. By then, it was just a black slimy mass, overtaken with maggots. From there, it all went downhill for me. I was petrified of all lizards, especially the transparent, croaking lizards."

Dr. Rose guided Natalie to float into the past, using her

time line, until she was above the incident that was the root cause of her fear. They set up the movie screen, and after about ten minutes of running her movie back and forth, Natalie no longer felt the intense fear. At the end of the session, Dr. Rose brought a lizard in a jar into the room. Natalie wrote about what happened next in a local newspaper:

"At first, I was a bit hesitant, then I took the bottle and stared at the underbelly of the creature. It just laid there, so I shook it a few times just to make sure it was alive, and it wiggled around a bit, and that was it. I felt absolutely nothing. Three nights later, I saw one running on the wall as I entered my house. Maybe I told myself that I shouldn't be afraid, but whatever it was, I watched it run right over my head and calmly went inside. Last week, I woke at about 3 a.m., and there was one in my bedroom. I just laid there looking at it as it chased moths, then I went back to sleep. I still don't like them, but I'm no longer terrified of them."

One of my students, Dr. Larry Momaya, who is a psychiatrist, actually became interested in NLP because of his own experience with an intense phobia and the MER Phobia Model:

In 2009, Dr. Momaya was on a first date with a woman he had recently met. As they walked to the restaurant, his date stepped off the curb to jaywalk, and he instinctively pulled her back. In that moment, a car screamed through a red light, hit another car, and flipped over three times. Larry froze and felt panicked as he watched the fire trucks and ambulance arrive. He was still visibly upset when they sat down to dinner.

His date (who had attended some of my trainings) asked him, "Would you like to get rid of this feeling?" While seated at dinner, she took Larry through the MER Phobia Model. He remembered an incident at his birthday party when he was five years old. Larry and the other children were running around the backyard. He threw a rock and unintentionally hit one of his friends. His friend's head began to bleed, and the little boy howled in pain and cried. The adults were alarmed and called an ambulance. As the ambulance arrived, sirens blaring, the mother of the little boy yelled at Larry, "You might have killed him!" From that traumatic event, Dr. Momaya had developed an intense fear of ambulances and sirens.

After several minutes of running the movie of this childhood event back and forth, Dr. Momaya felt calm and peaceful. It wasn't until days later that he actually heard an ambulance siren and noted, "The panic was definitely gone. I felt only a mild concern and compassion for that fellow human being who might be in trouble, but nothing more."

This amazing disappearance of his own phobia prompted Dr. Momaya to study MER for his practice. He was able to use the MER Phobia Model for one of his clients, whose phobia was more subtle:

Harry had come to see Dr. Momaya for help with weight loss. At 350 pounds, Harry was morbidly obese and had been diagnosed with Type II diabetes. Harry realized that he needed to make drastic changes for his health but had been unable to stick to a diet or exercise regimen. In one session, Dr. Momaya guided Harry through the MER process to release primary negative emotions and limiting beliefs. Harry left the session feeling confident that he could lose the weight he desired to lose.

Dr. Momaya didn't see Harry again until he came to the office eighteen months later. Harry had lost 120 pounds but was still about sixty pounds from his optimal weight. Harry told Dr. Momaya, "I was doing fine, then I hit a roadblock. I know I don't want to gain that weight back. But when I even think about losing more, I start to panic like something's wrong."

The roadblock turned out to be an intense fear that if he lost more weight, some terrible calamity would happen to his family. In unearthing the root cause of this fear, Harry remembered that decades before, after he had lost enough weight to be considered slim, his wife was diagnosed with cancer. Even though Harry knew consciously that losing weight could not have caused his wife's cancer, his unconscious still connected the two.

Dr. Momaya took Harry through the MER Phobia process: "Harry's fear dissipated within minutes. When I ran into him six months later, he had lost another forty pounds and was close to his goal weight."

10

Mental and Emotional Release and Other Disorders

My students and I have successfully used MER for a broad variety of psychological and physical disorders, everything from anorexia to high blood pressure to chronic anxiety to snoring. Rather than going into detail with any of these issues, I'll simply share some case studies to give you an idea of the breadth of concerns MER can address.

Severe Anxiety

Anxiety is basically defined as "belief that a future outcome will be negative." For specific anxieties, such as being anxious about an upcoming presentation or meeting, we use the time line process, which is slightly differently than the basic MER process. But anxiety that is chronic and pervasive usually stems from negative emotions or limiting decisions of events in the past.

A student of mine worked with a young woman we'll call Samantha. For years, Samantha had experienced extreme anxiety, to the extent that it created a phenomenon called "air hunger." People with this disorder get so anxious that they feel as if they can't breathe or get enough air. In Samantha's case, her air hunger would hit with no apparent rhyme or reason. Not knowing when it might hit again left her completely debilitated, unable to participate in normal activities, and she grew to have a massive fear of pain and death.

During her MER sessions, Samantha's unconscious tried to lead her to past lives or prior generations for the root cause of her issue. A staunch atheist, Samantha resisted this approach until her practitioner suggested that Samantha's unconscious mind was simply using these past-life or pre-birth experiences as metaphors to help solve her problem.

After releasing the five major negative emotions through MER, Samantha no longer experiences the air hunger with any regularity, and all of her former generalized anxiety is gone. She told her practitioner, "I've been to all kinds of therapists trying to deal with this. But this is the first time I've experienced any relief or improvement. I'm actually seeing results." Samantha continues to see her practitioner to release some of the limiting beliefs that have held her back. But after the initial work, she says she's thrilled to be a fully functional human being again.

Bedwetting

Bedwetting typically resolves itself over time, and research has shown that a child's bedwetting will stop around the same age that their parent's bedwetting stopped. When that's not the case, doctors prescribe drugs to minimize urine production at night or calm the bladder. But bedwetting often has underlying emotional components:

Another student of mine tells the story of a young client who was brought to her with a few presenting issues. Tama was bright eight-year-old who was falling behind in school. She reported that she had trouble concentrating during class and found it difficult to study and do schoolwork at home. Tama also talked about feeling awkward around other kids and felt hurt that she had no friends. When Tama left the room, her parents told my student that she had also started having frequent episodes of bedwetting.

With Tama's parents observing, my student guided the

little girl to identify her time line, which she did with ease. She practiced floating over her time line and then went through the process to release the major negative emotions with no difficulty. When the release was complete, Tama mentioned that she now felt "just fine" about school and was eager to get back to her classmates.

My student then asked Tama if there was any other problem she would like to resolve. Without saying what the problem was, Tama said yes. My student guided Tama to find the root cause of the problem and release it. Then they dealt with Tama's doubts that she could really change the problem and dropped the positive outcome into her future time line.

As my student reported, "The parents told me later that Tama's bedwetting is now extremely rare, and her focus dramatically improved in school. She also started making a few friends. An unexpected bonus was that, by observing how easily Tama released her issues, her parents felt much more relaxed and positive about their ability to be good parents."

Insomnia

Chronic insomnia is seen as very difficult to treat; medication is often only a Band-Aid. The medications typically used have side effects and are often highly addictive. And inadequate sleep over the long run can cause other problems, everything from depression to industrial accidents.

Mark was in his mid-fifties when he came to see one of my students. He complained of insomnia and claimed that he'd had problems sleeping as long as he could remember. In fact, Mark's mother said he hardly slept even as a small child.

Mark's insomnia had become worse and was associated with his diagnosis of bipolar disorder. After literally weeks of not sleeping, Mark had his first manic episode at age fifty-one. Since then, he had been treated for bipolar disorder with medication, and after five years on the medicine, his bipolar disorder seemed to be in remission.

However, Mark was still plagued by his inability to ever really sleep. He has undergone a sleep study, dozens of medications, and intensive psychotherapy, to no avail. He was happy that he could finally manage his bipolar disorder without medication but feared that his chronic insomnia might lead to another manic episode.

In Mark's first session, my student used MER to release his anger. His unconscious mind identified the root cause as a past life where Mark had been institutionalized and restrained in a straight-jacket. His anger kept him awake so he would be aware "of what they were doing to me." In subsequent sessions dealing with the other major negative emotions, Mark identified other past lives in which it was not safe to sleep.

Mark started getting more hours of sleep but still felt a lingering fear of really allowing himself to get a good night sleep. He uncovered a limiting decision from his early childhood: "If I sleep, I'll pee the bed." He'd had a bedwetting problem when he was about six and, from then on, decided that "sleep equaled bedwetting."

After releasing the limiting decision about bedwetting and sleep, predictably, Mark wet the bed on three occasions. But when his shame and guilt were released, he began sleeping soundly with no more incidents. He now sleeps six to seven hours per night, remains medication free, and has not had any recurrence of mania.

Bulimia

Chronic, persistent bulimia is usually treated with antidepressants and different forms of psychological talk therapy, such as cognitive behavior therapy (CBT), which tries to persuade clients to accept their body and learn to eat more nutritionally while learning to cope with current triggers (difficulties in current relationships, work- or school-related stress, etc.). But unless the root cause of the issue is unearthed, clients can easily relapse or exchange bulimia for a different symptom, such as substance abuse.

One of my students worked with Ellen, a very attractive young woman in her early twenties with a very pervasive eating disorder and problems with alcohol. Her mother (who had brought Ellen to my student) supported her financially; Ellen didn't work.

Ellen binged and purged many times daily. She said that this made her feel "disabled" and unable to work. With friends, she could keep up appearances, eating moderately and waiting until she got home to purge and binge. In the year before coming in for MER, Ellen started drinking excessively and even threatened suicide.

Coming in from out of town, Ellen was scheduled for a two-day breakthrough session. During the first session, Ellen identified one root cause event in which her father had left the family to work overseas for two years. In Ellen's young mind, he had left because she was "not good enough."

After the first session, Ellen left her hotel room and was out all night drinking. She called her mother in the morning, saying she was drunk and broke. Her mother picked her up and brought her to the second session.

As my student says, "This was a difficult two days. After day one, although we got some great results, Ellen told to her mother (not me) that she didn't think it worked. But today, about a year later, Ellen is in total remission. And she's recently been hired by an upscale department store as a personal shopper."

Sugar Addiction

Many scientists believe that sugar addiction is every bit as difficult to address as addiction to alcohol or heroin. Studies with rats and evidence in humans indicates that sugar affects the reward centers of the brain and creates a craving that is similar and at least as strong as addictive drugs. As with drugs or alcohol, not everyone who enjoys sugar becomes addicted. But for those who do, finding the root cause can be key to releasing the addiction.

One of my students worked with Raoul, a man in his mid-fifties who stood six foot four and weighed over three hundred pounds. He knew he needed to get in better shape for his health. Raoul was an active man and said he was willing to exercise more, "but I just can't lose weight, no matter what I do." His goal was to lose at least fifty pounds.

During the intake, Raoul talked about sugar, saying that he just couldn't go without it for very long. It became apparent that he'd had a vigorous addiction to sugar for as long as he could remember. "It doesn't work to use fruit or those sugar substitutes," he claimed. "I need the real thing." But he wanted to do whatever he could to eliminate his addiction to sugar and to lose weight.

In looking for the root cause, Raoul recalled an event when he was five years old. He wanted a cookie. But his mother, who was angry with him at the time, refused to give him one. He had a tantrum and from that moment decided that "love equals sweets." Once he released that limiting decision and the emotions around it, he was able to successfully complete a specific eating plan to detox from sugar. No longer attracted to it, Raoul was able to reach his weight goal in about six months and has maintained a healthy weight ever since.

Migraines

Migraines are extremely painful headaches that can last for hours or even days. They can be so severe that they're completely debilitating; all the sufferer can do is lie in a darkened room. Migraines can be triggered by a broad spectrum of issues, everything from hormonal changes to physical exertion to alcohol to certain foods. Milder migraines are typically treated with pain relievers like

Tylenol or ibuprofen. More severe chronic migraines are treated with a variety of drugs from botox to beta-blockers to certain antidepressants. According to the Mayo Clinic, "migraines can't be cured."[25]

Cheryl was referred to me years ago by her MD because none of the medication they had tried could get her migraines under control. She experienced chronic migraines that incapacitated her and prevented her from doing anything. Cheryl's MD had told her, "This is beyond my scope and is more likely stress related due to your hostile work environment." Cheryl had been told over and over by a number of people that her job was too stressful and she should quit it to preserve her sanity and her physical health. But she refused, saying, "I make way too much money to let a little stress interfere."

Cheryl began the session with me by stating that "under no circumstances" was she going to quit her job, adding, "If you even suggest it, I promise that I won't pay you." Though I rarely let a client dictate terms like that, for some reason, I let Cheryl slide. As we got further into the issue, she expressed her anger toward her boss, who consistently made sexual advances toward her. We traced this back to a root cause event and released all of the negative emotions surrounding that event.

At the end of the session, I always assign a task. A task is something the client must do in order to solidify the release work. But I looked at Carol and said, "I always assign a task, but I am not going to assign you one." She asked me why, and I reminded her of the terms she set at the beginning. "Instead of a task," I said, "I am just going to ask you what you think you should do to solidify your release."

She looked sheepishly at her feet and said, "I should quit my job."

---

[25]   http://www.mayoclinic.org/diseases-conditions/
migraine-headache/basics/treatment/con-20026358

We both laughed, and I said, "Well, since you said it, not me, you can still pay me."

Not only did Cheryl's migraines stop completely, she quit her job and found a better job with less stress and more money.

Impotence

Erectile dysfunction may have physical causes (such as kidney disease, high blood pressure, or diabetes) as well as psychological causes (such as depression, stress, or anxiety). Experts believe impotence affects between ten and fifteen million American men.[26] Today, treatments for impotence range from drugs like Viagra and Cialis to surgery to hormonal therapy to counseling.

Stan was one of my very first clients, many years ago. When he sat down to do the MER process with me, I asked, "Why are you here?"

He responded with, "All women hate me."

I remember this distinctly; my response was, "How do you know that all three billion women on this planet hate you? Do all three billion hate you?"

After a few minutes of talking it through, Stan finally narrowed it down to "all the women I've been with hate me." He also confessed that he was suffering from sexual dysfunction. In every relationship he'd ever had, he was unable to perform sexually. He placed the blame on his partners.

After some simple investigation during his detailed personal history, we unearthed that Stan had significant anger toward his mother, a woman who was very promiscuous. I'd never seen a case where the symptom was so directly linked to its root cause. Even Steve looked at me at one point and said, "No wonder why I don't want to be with any woman except the ones I can't have."

After releasing his anger, he recognized that women didn't

---

[26] http://www.rightdiagnosis.com/artic/impotence_niddk.htm

hate him after all. But he felt an overwhelming sadness and guilt about his past behavior. We released those emotions as well. In our follow-up session a week later, Stan reported that for the first time, he had been able to be sexually intimate with his girlfriend. "It wasn't up to the level of performance I want yet," he admitted, "but it's a start."

Thirty-Seven-Year-Old Virgin

Celibacy can be a life choice for a number of reasons. But for people who desire a sexual relationship, involuntary celibacy can be very painful and invariably has a root cause: a limiting belief or negative emotion that can be released. The following example was sent to me by one of my students:

"Charlie was thirty-seven when he called me and said that he had never had sex. He claimed that his interest in pornography and masturbation had ruined his ability to function normally with a woman. He was pretty sure he was heterosexual because he felt attracted to women. From our phone calls in preparation for his visit, I assumed Charlie would be unattractive, maybe morbidly obese, or in some way very unappealing.

"I was totally wrong. Charlie is not only in great shape physically (he works in construction and is a tri-athlete), but I'm betting most women would describe him as very handsome. Charlie said he'd never been abused sexually. He didn't do drugs and drank only socially. Though he described himself as shy in general, he was able to interact socially and professionally with women

"Charlie worried that his frequent masturbation had ruined his ability to have sex, that he might have damaged himself somehow. And because his masturbation sessions were furtive and fast, he worried that, if he did get up the courage to have sex with a woman, he might have a premature ejaculation and ruin the whole experience. He had started masturbating with pornography at fifteen.

So his self-perpetuating cycle of worry and fear had been running for more than twenty years.

"Charlie lived in another state, so we arranged to do three sessions spaced out over three months. We used MER to clear negative emotions of anger, fear, hurt, sadness, and guilt. Next we tackled his limiting decisions like 'I'm too shy to be with a woman,' 'I'm a bad lover,' 'I'll never be with anyone,' and 'Masturbation has ruined me.' We also worked on his internal conflict that part of him is a nice guy and another part is a sex maniac. We resolved this conflict using the NLP Parts Integration technique.

"Charlie recently emailed me to refer someone to me. He told me that he's no longer a virgin. He's been in a relationship for over six months, and they're planning to move in together. And he says he's learned how to 'be a good lover.'"

11

Mental and Emotional Release to Enhance Life

Though people often talk about MER's amazing results with serious clinical conditions like PTSD or anorexia, my students and I have also experienced thousands of success stories from people who were "fine" or even very accomplished, yet they still felt blocked somehow and were not getting all they wanted from life. Some of these are like so many people: They were "getting by" but not feeling fulfilled or inspired. Others had even achieved great success in one or two areas of life but felt something was lacking in others.

The main issues that keep most people up at night are in the areas of health (in this country, "health" often translates into weight issues), money, career, and intimate relationships. So I've gathered some case studies in those areas from my students to illustrate the dramatic shifts and empowerment possible through MER.

Health

Obesity is rampant in this country. Have you ever wondered why a diet works for some people and not for others? Or why willpower alone just doesn't cut it for most people? Many people who truly desire to lose weight end up on the roller coaster of yo-yo dieting, failing time and time again.

Typically, this means that their sincere efforts are being sabotaged by limiting decisions or negative emotions held in the unconscious mind. As I learned back in school, the number one factor determining if a diet is going to work is the thing between your ears: your mind, or more accurately, your baggage (or lack thereof).

One of my students worked with a client who came to him to resolve her weight issues. Eileen had been overweight most of her life. But by the time she hit her late fifties, this excess weight was beginning to take its toll and was affecting her ability to do her job as a birthing coach. Though she enjoyed her work, Eileen felt that most of her life was "blah," and she didn't have much of a social life. "I know I use food to feel better," she confessed. "But I'm ashamed that I've let myself get this heavy."

Eileen had been given up for adoption when she was very young and ended up with adoptive parents who were cold and verbally abusive. Her brief marriage was an unhappy one. "My husband sounded like my parents," she said, "always critical. I didn't like it, but somehow I thought I deserved the criticism." It was after her divorce that Eileen gained enough weight to be considered morbidly obese.

During her MER sessions, Eileen recognized that she felt to blame for being abandoned as a child. As she released the anger, sadness, and guilt of that event, she reported feeling at peace with herself and a new acceptance of the path her life had taken. "I may have made some mistakes," she said, "but I deserved to be treated better. And I deserve to treat myself better as well."

In the weeks and months after her sessions, Eileen found it naturally easier to stick to a healthier diet and even started an exercise program. "Now what 'feels good' is not scarfing down a quart of Chunky Monkey," she said, "but taking good care of my body." The weight is slowly coming off, and she feels much more energetic and excited about her life.

Overeating, like drug and alcohol abuse, can often be a

form of self-medicating, as with this client of another one of my students:

Diane, a computer technician in her late thirties, was not only overweight, her eating patterns had become obsessive. She kept stashes of her favorite foods, chocolate and peanut butter, everywhere she went: her car, her desk at work, even in her gym bag. She said, "It's so bad that I actually start feeling anxious when the peanut butter jar gets low. I've actually left work in the middle of the day to get more so I wouldn't be without it."

Diane's work required a lot of concentration. But she found herself becoming distracted by her obsession with food and unable to focus on the task at hand. Her performance became so erratic that her supervisor advised her to seek counseling if she wished to keep her position.

In her first session with my student, Diane talked about her lack of self-confidence: "I'm in a field that is dominated by men. I feel like I have to watch my back all the time with those guys, like I'm never quite good enough." She knew her eating was a problem and had tried to control it, but that made her feel anxious and "painfully deprived," so the eating continued.

Interestingly, even though Diane did not particularly believe in past lives, her unconscious led her to various prebirth experiences as the root cause of her issues. At the end of the MER session, she felt much more in control and mentally focused. In follow-up sessions, my student addressed the specific foods she had craved and some of her limiting beliefs about her abilities on the job. By the end, Diane's newfound confidence felt solid, and she announced, "I can do anything."

Not every weight issue is a lifelong issue. Specific situations can trigger dormant patterns and turn a healthy eater and exerciser into an overeater:

Susan was in her late sixties, a retired CFO for a well-known regional real estate firm. Though her career had been very successful, she had experienced three early marriages that had failed and had remained single since her mid-forties. Her children had grown to be well-adjusted adults, and she looked forward to having grandchildren.

Though she had been slim her entire life, Susan had gained forty pounds within the past two years, right after her son's wedding. This prompted her to seek the help of my student. She said, "I have never had an issue with eating right and exercising. But now I find myself overeating almost every night and drinking much more wine than I ever have. And I can't seem to stop."

Susan's childhood had been difficult, with a father who had abused alcohol and was physically violent. She left the home as soon as she was eighteen and successfully worked her way through college. As she discussed her past, she admitted to feeling very disappointed by the way her life had turned out; she said, "I feel like I should be grateful for all I've been able to accomplish. But honestly, I just feel empty."

As Susan experienced the MER process, she was able to release the hurt and betrayal she had felt in her marriages. She was also able to distinguish between inappropriate, unwarranted emotion with warranted emotion. She said, "I was hanging on to emotions from the past that were robbing me of my enjoyment in the present. I still can get angry or hurt, but it moves through me quickly now. I can choose how or if I want to respond to what happens. It's no longer a knee-jerk reaction."

Since her sessions, Susan feels much more energetic and alive. She's resumed her active physical life, is well on her way to dropping the weight she had gained, and no longer feels the need to eat at night. She's back to drinking only an occasional glass of wine and is even open to the possibility of a new romantic relationship.

Clients also use MER in preparation for treatments or surgeries, as the client with cancer I mentioned in chapter 2:

Paula was one of the students during my Master

Practitioner training. During this training, students exchange MER sessions, switching between the roles of practitioner and client. In her mid-sixties, Paula was retired and scheduled to undergo bilateral hip replacement surgery. In her role as client during the MER practice session, Paula asked to focus on health and well-being to maximize the chances of having a successful outcome from her upcoming surgery.

During Paula's MER session, she had no startling or surprising revelations. Guided by her fellow student, she released any fears and doubts about the procedure and placed her desired outcome in her time line in the future.

A month later, she reported back to the student who had acted as her practitioner: "I was completely pain-free from the very first moment after the surgery, which the nurses said is unheard of. I actually walked that very next day. And my physiotherapist said I had the best scores for recovery of anyone she's ever seen in her eleven years of practice. I even outscored people who had just one hip replaced."

Career and Finances

I frequently give seminars focused specifically on money because so many people are frustrated that they aren't where they want to be financially or feel very insecure when it comes to money. It's an issue that inevitably comes up in every training and seminar I give.

Years ago, I used to run a different type of seminar to introduce MER to new students, and that's where I met Amar. He had immigrated to Canada from India with a wife and two daughters but nothing in his pocket. While he came to North America with a ton of hope and a burning desire to make a better life for his family, he also came with a lot of fear around his ethnicity as well as his ability to speak English.

During his first months in his new country, Amar felt at odds with the culture and struggled to make ends meet. He was very close to giving up when he saw an advertisement

126

for one of the weekend events we ran at that time. During the event, along with the rest of the group, Amar went through the MER process to release his negative emotions (he was actually one of the subjects we used to demonstrate how to release limiting decisions). At that time, Amar shared with the group that he had to borrow the $300 to attend the event and that he had high hopes. At the end of the event, he set his goals, as we'd shown him how to do in the seminar. Then he put his workbook away and did not think much about it.

One year later, Amar was cleaning out his bookshelf because he'd just bought a new house for his family. He found the workbook from our training. Curious, he flipped through it and then read all the goals he had set. To his astonishment, he had hit them all. He had made $1 million in that year. He had purchased a house for his family, and he was sending his daughters to college, just as stated in his goals. He recognized that he had been able to do this because he was finally free of his limitations. He immediately called our office. He signed up for all our trainings, and he brought his wife and daughters along. For years after, Amar shared his story in our groups and inspired others to release their baggage.

Many of us recognize that we have more potential than we're able to tap. My students and I have had numerous clients who by all measures are very successful, yet they know that they could achieve so much more.

Beth was a well-regarded public speaker who also coached executives of small to medium-size companies. In her mid-sixties, Beth came to one of my students after many years of various forms of psychotherapy. She'd joined AA to overcome a drinking problem and remained sober for over twenty years. But Beth felt that she had never been able to release the baggage—especially the guilt—from her past. "I've worked with so many different therapists," she said, "some of them for years. But they just kept dragging me through the muck and the mire. Nothing ever really changed for me."

Beth felt that her years of therapy had actually undermined her sense of self-worth and confidence: *"Maybe I wasn't so confident before. But most of them made me feel even worse. In fact, one therapist was so critical of anything I did, I became terrified to make any decisions on my own."* Despite her lack of self-esteem and confidence, Beth built a very successful career. *"But I'm tired of the struggle and carrying around so much old baggage,"* she said.

Beth had four sessions of MER altogether, and she was thrilled at how quickly her years of baggage disappeared. After the first session, she noticed how much more comfortable she was with her very wealthy clients. *"I always felt like an outsider. Now I just feel like I belong."* After the second session, she was able to connect more intimately with her adult daughter. And by the third session, she was making plans to expand her business into a territory that had previously seemed out of her league.

"The difference between this [NLP and MER] and the other therapies I tried is that it seems to work from the inside out," she said. *"Rather than being force-fed to feel or think differently, it's as if I'm coming to those conclusions myself. I'm naturally feeling differently, and I'm getting positive results in my work and with my relationships without even trying."*

Often, a career is stalled out not by your performance but by your *perception* of your performance. This was the case with one of my students' clients, Deidre.

Deidre, college guidance counselor and life coach, sought help from one of my students, claiming she lacked concentration and focus, was disorganized, and was very easily distracted. But as she described her life, it became clear that she was highly organized and doing an amazing job juggling all that was on her plate. A wife and mother of two active youngsters, Deidre was not only assisting with her aging father but also had a full client load in both her counseling position and her coaching business. On top of this, she assisted several local nonprofits in organizing their fundraising events.

During her MER sessions, Deidre's unconscious identified a variety of past life events as root cause events. In one, she was a soldier who left his family and died in battle. He had not only failed at his mission, he had also left his family without protection. Deidre was able to connect this event to her present-day anxious habit of saying a "meaningful good-bye" to each family member whenever she left, "just in case." As she released the guilt and fear of this past event, she felt more at peace in the present.

In another root cause event, Deidre was a leader whose misjudgment had resulted in tragedy and cost many lives. In her present life, that incident had carried over to become a fear of making any kind of mistake. During the session, as she released her fear and sadness over the event, she felt a great sense of relief. "It's as if I can breathe for the first time," she said. "The learning I got was that 'if you don't make mistakes, you won't be able to realize your greatness.'"

In her follow-up session, Deidre reported that she felt much more balanced and at ease. "I'm probably doing just as much, but I don't feel the stress and anxiety I used to feel. And I'm so much more willing to try things out of my comfort zone. If I blow it, that's just life. No big deal."

In some instances, the client's relationship with money itself can become an obstacle to having a fulfilling career, as in Jamie's case.

Jamie had grown up in a blue collar family who had high hopes for her future career. The family sacrificed to help her through college and eventually medical school. She worked hard through school and during her residency, and became a very well-regarded pediatrician in a busy hospital.

She married an attorney, and they quickly had two healthy children. But even though Jamie made well over

$200,000 per year and her husband earned a good income as well, Jamie felt perpetually afraid of "becoming homeless and destitute." Though she and her husband wanted to expand their family, Jamie refused to consider buying a larger house or replacing their decades-old cars.

Jamie initially came to my student to overcome her persistent anorexia. After successfully using MER to resolve her eating issues, she asked about using the same process for a few themes in her life that were "annoying but not life threatening." She talked about her fear of ending up in poverty. She also mentioned that though she'd always wanted to build her own private practice, she was terrified to leave the security of her hospital paycheck.

Jamie ended up releasing several limiting beliefs about money. She assumed these beliefs were from her parents. But when asked about the root cause, she was shown a particular past life (though Jamie did not necessarily believe that past lives exist) where "standing out from the crowd" as a success was punished by persecution and losing everything. She was able to release all the negative emotions and limiting decisions around this event.

Jamie and her husband now live in a beautiful, much larger home. She has not only established her own practice but has opened a clinic that is quite profitable. "I'm actually making more money doing what I love," she said, "and am no longer afraid to pursue what makes me happy."

Of course, the areas of our lives spill over into one another. The following case is of a student of mine whose relationship issues negatively impacted her career and ability to make money.

Patricia was an attractive young woman in her mid-twenties when she came first to my practitioners training then to the Master Practitioner training a few months later. She was attracted to NLP because she was starting to "question whether anyone could ever really be happy."

Several years previously, Patricia had been abducted

and beaten by a boyfriend she was trying to break up with. He threatened to kill her if she told anyone what happened, so she kept silent. But when he started stalking her a year later, she went to the police. The experience only got more painful as Patricia had to describe the incident and relive it in court. The ex-boyfriend got off with no punishment, she lost friends and family who didn't believe her story, and she was sent to a therapist "who only made it worse."

Patricia moved away to start fresh. She learned to meditate and started attending a church, both of which helped to some extent. But she seemed to encounter similar situations with the men in her life and even entered a male-dominated field. Finally, after months working with a verbally abusive male supervisor, Patricia fell into a deep depression. Struggling at her commission-only job, Patricia was making only $1,000 per week, barely enough to cover her living expenses. She was dating a nice man but felt her resentment kept them from becoming close. "I started to feel, 'What's the point?'" she said. "'Why even try?'"

Patricia attended my NLP practitioner training. Immediately afterwards, her commissions tripled. A few months later, she attended my Master Practitioner training, where students exchange MER sessions. In her role as the client, Patricia released negative emotions and the trauma from her experience with the ex-boyfriend. By the end of the session, she said she felt "comfortable in her own skin," that she could express herself freely and relax for the first time in years. "Happiness is a natural state," she said. "We all have an inalienable right to it."

Months later, she says that her income continues to increase, and she is totally comfortable with her male co-workers and clients. Her relationship is "amazing" and fulfilling: "I've learned that you teach people how to treat you."

Relationships

Fulfilling relationships are a key part of a healthy, happy life. Yet too many people seem unable to create the relationships they desire and deserve. As Eugene Nathaniel Butler says, "Embarking on a relationship is like setting off at sea in a sailboat for two. Too much baggage from the past will sink it."

A student of mine told me about a recent client, a man in his late thirties named Justin. Justin had just ended a marriage with a woman who had treated him very badly. Several months later, he met a wonderful woman online, and they started dated. But though Justin felt that he had "moved on" after his divorce, he was having trouble being fully present in his new relationship. "I feel conflicted," he said, "but I don't know why."

After releasing the major emotions around relationships, Justin felt much more open and free. But he had unearthed a limiting belief that "it's just not okay to get divorced," and that belief was still present. My student guided him to find the root cause of this belief, and Justin was surprised to find that it was five generations prior. Through the MER process, he was finally able to release that belief. Six months later, he reported that his relationship had improved dramatically right after the session and that their loving connection continued to deepen.

Limiting beliefs about relationships come in many forms, as in the next case:

Another student of mine worked with an ambitious young career-oriented woman, Amy, who had broken up with her longtime boyfriend, Gil, the year before. The break-up was hard but amicable, and Gil and Amy kept in touch. Amy had come to see my student because she felt there was a real possibility that the two of them could get back together, adding, "But I'm pretty sure the things that I do and my energy overall is blocking us from ever having true love and intimacy."

During the intake process, one of Amy's limiting beliefs came to light: that accepting help from a man meant she was incapable of doing things for herself. As a child, she had watched her mother sacrifice her career to become a good "CEO wife" to her father. "Mom knows nothing about business," she said, "and Dad likes it that way." Amy recognized that this belief was not only getting in the way of her relationship, it also made her doubt her own ability to succeed.

Five months after releasing this belief through MER, not only did Amy move in with her boyfriend, she also went back to school to get the training she needed to pursue the career in public relations she'd always wanted.

Remember that old saying that "you marry your mother [or your father]"? Sometimes, that's *not* the best idea:

Another client, Claire, came to one of my students to get rid of her constant anger. "I hear you have some technique that can help me let go of my rage," she said. "I am one pissed-off black woman!" Now forty-five, Claire had been married once for many years. After her divorce, she had several difficult, short-lived relationships. Claire had a daughter who would soon be leaving for college. "I don't want to be alone," she said, "but I'll never let another man in my life to hurt me again. Maybe I'll just get a dog."

During MER, Claire recognized the connection between her rage and her biological father, an abusive alcoholic who had deserted the family when Claire was only three, adding, "It looks like I've been attracting the same kind of man as dear old Dad."

After releasing her anger, Claire felt a great deal of sadness and fear, which she released as well. Over the next few sessions, she released the many limiting decisions she had made about men and spent some time figuring out better strategies for picking a potential mate. She did get herself a dog and ultimately met and married a very nice man. "He treats me in a way I've never been treated," she said. *"Now I'm making up for all the time I wasted with the losers."*

Of course, we have relationships beyond our significant others. One student was concerned not only about his relationship with his spouse but also his relationship with his children:

When Brian came to my NLP Practitioners training, he had been on the self-discovery, self-improvement journey for a few years. He had been raised in an addiction-run, abusive household and had never been able to find closure, no matter what outlet he used for therapy.

His main symptom was a very short fuse. As he got older, he tried to "bottle it up," which only made his anger more explosive when he finally let loose. "When I exploded," he said, "it's like I was two people at the same time. The whole time I'd be thinking, This isn't fixing anything. There has to be a better way to handle this. *But I couldn't stop it." With a high-pressure job and three boisterous children, Brian found that his anger was triggered more frequently and with hardly any provocation. "I knew I had to change for myself, for my wife, and for my children, but I felt I had exhausted all other options."*

During the training weekend, Brian began to feel a little bit of hope. On the last day, I used Brian and his anger issue to demonstrate MER. He said he felt better immediately after, but he still had his doubts. "The exercise seemed far too simplistic and minimal to have any kind of long-term impact," he said. "How could it change who I'd been my entire life?"

Brian wrote to me to explain what happened next: "After leaving the course I went about my life not really noticing much change. I had new knowledge but I didn't see how I truly had changed. About three or four weeks after leaving the course I ran into a situation at work that built into a plethora of triggers for me. It's like the universe was giving me a test.

"After four consecutive horrible days at work, right when I was almost at the end of a project, Murphy's Law kicked in. Everything that could've possibly gone wrong went wrong: every one of my pet peeves! When the entire situation imploded (which was long past the point I normally would've exploded), I had no reaction. I just rolled with it like it was part of the process.

"I even cracked a joke! I noticed I didn't get a response from a colleague who usually laughs at everything. I noticed his bewildered look and realized what was happening. I began laughing because I realized how much I had changed and how good that change felt. My friend actually began to panic, thinking I was having a nervous breakdown.

"Professionally, that was one of the worst weeks I've ever had, but it ended with one of the highest points of my life. I've never felt more empowered than I did in that moment or more grateful."

12

Recent MER Research

As I mentioned in the introduction, a couple of my students and colleagues recently completed professional studies on MER. Documenting the efficacy of any psychotherapeutic technique is difficult. Critics point to the subjective nature of such studies, and the numerous variables across patients make it hard to quantify results.

That said, the study Dr. Patrick Scott conducted over a two-year period comparing cognitive behavioral therapy alone to CBT combined with MER revealed a significant difference: Patients who were given the combination of CBT and MER returned to a higher level of functioning much more quickly and (as of this writing, five years after the study) had no relapses or re-hospitalizations. And the study Dr. Tracey Coley conducted with at-risk youth in Jamaica illustrates the power of MER to change the very course of a young person's life.

MER Efficacy Study in Nevada

The first study[27] in this chapter was conducted by Dr. Patrick Ross Scott.[28] Since learning Mental and Emotional Release therapy in 2007, Dr. Scott has considered MER to

---

[27] "The Efficacy of Time Empowerment Techniques in the Treatment of Depressive Disorders (More Recently Known as Mental and Emotional Release Therapy)."

[28] Patrick Ross Scott, PhD, LCSW, DCSW, FAPA.

be his "go to" technique. "It's straightforward and targeted," he said. "Patients don't have to relive any traumas from the past to resolve them, and they don't have to go into deep hypnotic trance. For 80 to 85 percent of my patients, MER gives tremendous relief from their symptoms in the very first session."

Based on his own success with the treatment, Dr. Scott was surprised that MER therapy was not more widely known and used in the therapeutic community. "I know that we therapists tend to stick with the techniques that are most familiar to us," he said. "But when you find something that can be this effective, it's too bad that more professionals don't have it within their toolkit."

So beginning in October of 2008, Dr. Scott and his team conducted a retrospective two-year study to quantify the benefits and effectiveness of MER. This study was used as the basis of his doctoral dissertation. The goal was to compare results in patients who had received MER therapy in combination with CBT to patients who had received CBT treatment alone.

Cognitive behavioral therapy is a system of psychotherapy that works with maladaptive thought and behavioral patterns. In CBT, it is believed that negative patterns can lie dormant until they are triggered by a significant (or in some cases, seemingly insignificant) life event. In CBT, the therapist assists patients in identifying these negative patterns and bringing them to conscious awareness. The patient is encouraged to adopt new patterns that are more effective and positive. CBT requires active participation from the patient, as does MER. (If patients are severely depressed or so despondent and lethargic that they are unable to engage in conversation, hospitalization or medication management might be required before either CBT or MER can begin.)

For example, a depressed patient might have thought patterns that are catastrophic and lead to rash decisions and behaviors, such as, "I'm falling behind on my bills, so I'll just be homeless and live on the street." Basically, in CBT, the therapist would encourage the patient to look at that assumption (late payments equals homelessness) and develop more positive thought patterns, such as, "I am falling behind so I need to find a better way to handle my finances."

Dr. Scott shares the story of Joey, a man in his late twenties who was out on parole after three years in prison:

"While incarcerated, Joey had been raped. Ever since then, he had shown signs of depression that showed up as anger. Whenever Joey felt anxious or fearful, he got into the habit of getting drunk and going from bar to bar to do some 'gay bashing,' assaulting just about anyone who crossed his path. He was referred to me to learn to manage his anger.

"Working with Joey using CBT, we first identified his catastrophic thinking: 'I don't feel safe so I'm going to hurt people that have hurt me.' From there, we helped Joey find better thoughts when he felt anxious, like, 'I am safe in my own skin. I can make choices.' Then we gave him alternative behaviors such as going for a run or calling his counselor when he felt fearful."

The negative thought patterns could also be things like erroneous assumptions ("He didn't take out the trash so he doesn't love me"), broad generalizations ("People like me never get ahead"), or inappropriate personalization ("It must be my fault that the project came out so poorly"). In CBT, any of these patterns would first be identified so the patient is conscious of them and then replaced with patterns that are more positive and empowering.

Participants

The study involved over nine hundred subjects. Of those, the majority were patients of Heads Up Guidance & Wellness Centers in downtown Las Vegas, which offer individual, family, and group counseling to those who have no access to mental health services. These clinics are specifically geared to assisting individuals and families to move out of public housing and into more independent living. Many of the residents in the public housing projects had lived in poverty for decades and even generations. But the patients who came in for treatment, though low income, often unemployed, and struggling, tended to be more motivated to address their issues and move "up and out."

Less than two hundred of the subjects in this study were patients at Summerlin Health & Wellness Centers, which serve a demographic that includes the more middle-class and upper-middle-class suburbs of the Las Vegas metropolitan area. Patients in these clinics ran the gamut from active military to professionals, many of whom were facing unemployment and severe economic challenges for the first time due to the severe economic recession at that time. For instance, one patient in this study had spent his entire thirty-year career as an executive in the gambling industry. In his last position, he had made $500,000 per year. When he came for therapy, after three years of unemployment, he was working as a security guard, making $12 per hour.

During the timeframe of this study, Las Vegas led the nation in home foreclosures, personal bankruptcies, unemployment, murder-suicides, women killed by men, and per-capita residence of registered sex offenders. In addition, the city's suicide rate is three times that of the national average. Clearly, the area has a prevalence of mental health issues, and both the Summerlin Centers and Heads Up Centers are extremely active.

Of the 922 patients in the study, 377 had been diagnosed with major depressive disorder[29] (commonly referred to as clinical depression), and 541 had been diagnosed with adjustment disorder accompanied by depression. An adjustment disorder is a stress-related mental illness. It

---

[29] See chapter 6 for a discussion of depression.

is typically caused by stressful life changes such as work problems, going away to school, an illness, a divorce, or the loss of a loved one. During the timeframe of this study, stress caused by the economic downturn—foreclosures, unemployment, bankruptcies—were very common.

Normally, people are able to adjust to such changes within a few months. However, in adjustment disorders, the patient continues to feel anxious or depressed, or even have thoughts of suicide. Normal daily routines may seem overwhelming, and patients may make rash decisions. Basically, they are unable to tap their natural ability to adjust to the changes in their lives.

Darren, a forty-year-old customer service rep, is a classic example of an adjustment disorder. In the year prior to his entering therapy, both of Darren's parents had died, his wife had left him, his teenaged children had cut off all contact with him, and he had lost his house to foreclosure. Obviously, anyone in Darren's situation would have felt grief and distress. But after a year, his emotional state was beginning to affect his work and ability to cope with life in general. The goal of his treatment was not to erase his emotions but to make them less intense so he could process them and move forward.

Along with clinical depression or adjustment disorder with depression, many patients in the study had substance abuse issues or chronic pain, and 36 percent were on psychotropic drugs such as antidepressants or antianxiety medications.

Sherry, a sixty-seven-year-old grandmother, was not atypical. She had suffered trauma and sexual abuse as a young woman and so had been on Prozac for over twenty years. At the beginning of her treatment, she was on a daily dosage of 40mg of Prozac along with pain medications for her severe arthritis. Sherry received both MER and CBT, and by the end of her treatment, her Prozac had been cut in half to 20mg.

Survey and Results

Of the 922 patients in the study, 99 had been treated using the combination of MER and CBT. The remaining 823 had received CBT only (the control group). All treatment was on an outpatient basis. The control group (CBT-only) received more than two or more forty-five-minute session of cognitive behavioral therapy by a licensed intern therapist or practicum student. The experimental group received sessions of CBT as well as at least two sessions of MER therapy with Dr. Scott.

The results revealed that patients in the experimental group experienced relief from their symptoms in 37 percent fewer sessions than patients in the control group. Patients in the experimental group averaged five MER sessions to achieve complete remission of their symptoms, and no patient in that group required more than eight.

To illustrate the contrast, Dr. Scott shared two case studies where the patients shared similar diagnoses and backgrounds. Noah was in the control group and had received CBT, only while Roger had received both MER and CBT.

At the time of his therapy, Noah was nineteen. He was brought to therapy by his mother, who complained that he was uncooperative, belligerent, and unable to keep a job. Noah said that he felt "pissed off all the time" and that nothing interested him; he resented his parents' rules and restrictions. After twelve weekly sessions of therapy, he reported feeling much better. His mother said he was much more cooperative and was communicating more positively with the family. However, six months after his therapy, Noah was arrested for assault. Though he had good CBT tools he could use to make better choices in normal circumstances, the stress of an argument with a friend had set him off again.

Twenty-six-year-old Roger had similar issues with controlling his anger and frustration around his family, along with a gambling addiction. He worked as a parking valet in one of the casinos and rarely made it home at night without having dropped all of his tip money at the tables. Unable to afford his own place, Roger was living with his younger brother, and the two were constantly fighting. After six sessions of MER, Roger's urge to gamble had disappeared. He was no longer fighting with his brother and had saved enough money to move out on his own.

Interestingly, patients in the CBT combined with MER group *continued* with their therapy even after initial symptoms had disappeared. It appears that after immediate relief from their depressive symptoms, these patients felt hopeful and continued to seek treatment to work on other areas of their lives. This is in stark contrast to the control group, where an overwhelming majority had fewer than four total sessions before dropping out, with no documented improvement of their symptoms.

While the study did not specifically track the condition of patients after their therapy, Dr. Scott's research team could find no cases of relapse, recidivism, or rehospitalization in the group that received MER. In contrast, the control group experienced a 29 percent occurrence of relapse or recidivism and an 11 percent occurrence of rehospitalization for psychiatric reasons during the two-year study period.

I talked to Dr. Scott about a few case studies that are representative of the results patients in the experimental group achieved:

When Jillian came in for therapy, she was thirty-three and a successful attorney in a large law firm. Though she had been in and out of therapy for many years, she appeared to those around her to be happy and on top of her game. But the discovery that her husband of four years was cheating on her brought many of her past issues to a head. "When Jillian came to see me," Dr. Scott reported, "she and her husband had separated. She wasn't sleeping, and she couldn't eat so had lost a lot of weight. She constantly felt anxious and depressed and was having difficulty concentrating at work. Though she was adamant that her marriage was over, she wanted to 'heal and forgive,' and she certainly wanted to feel and function better."

Because of the urgency of her situation and her familiarity with therapy, Dr. Scott and Jillian decided to do the intensive MER breakthrough process: a five-hour session in one day that encompassed work that he would normally perform over at least five weeks. "I don't recommend this for everyone," he said. "For some people, it's just too much too quickly. But Jillian is very self-aware and receptive."*

Within the session, Jillian's difficult childhood came to light. For as long as she could remember, her mother had been in and out of mental hospitals. Her father had been physically abusive to her mother and had abandoned the family when Jillian was six. So she grew up with no father and a "crazy, dysfunctional" mother.

"I took Jillian through the Mental and Emotional Release process to deal with all five basic negative emotions," he explained. "Then Jillian noticed that, despite her previous experiences in therapy, she felt certain specific incidents needed to be resolved. So we used her time line to address those also."*

The result? A few weeks after the session, Jillian and her husband entered couples therapy to work on their issues. Within a few months, they had recommitted to their marriage. And two years later, they celebrated the birth of their first child. During that time, Jillian also was made a partner at her firm based on her outstanding performance, and she formed a more positive relationship with her mother.

"Jillian never regretted her prior years of therapy and felt she got value from them," Dr. Scott said. "But she credits the MER session with clearing the issues that had held her back from relating authentically with her husband and her mother, and feeling confident and powerful at work."*

Dr. Scott's second case study had a course of therapy

that was more common to most of the other patients in the experimental group:

Andrew, a twenty-two-year-old mechanic in the Air Force, sought treatment to get a better handle on his anger. "He came to me saying that he was frustrated at work and took that frustration out on his girlfriend when he got home," Dr. Scott said. "It had never escalated to physical violence, but their arguments were increasingly frequent and intense, and Andrew was afraid of what might happen if he was pushed too far."

Along with his anger, Andrew had classic signs of depression: feelings of sadness and poor self-esteem, and he was drinking alcohol to excess more often than previously. He had also gained forty pounds in the prior few months and said that he felt distracted and unmotivated at work. "As we talked in that first session," Dr. Scott said, "Andrew mentioned that he had felt similarly years before, right after a motor vehicle accident in which a good friend had been killed."

Andrew's first few sessions with Dr. Scott focused on building rapport and beginning his CBT. He was told to start tracking his negative emotions and what seemed to trigger them. "By session 4, Andrew told me that he felt worse than ever. He could see how bad his boundaries were and said he felt like 'a doormat.' This led to feeling rotten about himself which then turned into anger and even more fights with his girlfriend."

In the fifth session, they began working with MER therapy, and Andrew felt that his negative emotions were significantly lessened by the seventh session. "But at that point," Dr. Scott explained, "he said he needed to deal with the accident that had killed his friend. Andrew confessed that he had been driving drunk that night and had fallen asleep at the wheel, causing the accident that killed his friend. Prior to the MER release work, he'd never been able to tell the truth of that night to anyone." In that session, Dr.

Scott took Andrew through the MER Phobia Model to deal with the trauma, guilt, and pain Andrew felt from that event.

"Our last session was just a debriefing," he said. "Andrew said he felt like an entirely different person and that everyone around him said he was just like his old self. I saw him months later on the base. He said he and his girlfriend were planning their wedding. Andrew actually thanked me for our work together in front of several other guys—very unusual for a guy in the military."

Jamaican Study of At-Risk Children

"Miss, do you know that I don't understand what happened to me? I used to fight every day at school; it wasn't because anyone was troubling me—I just felt haunted, and everything other people did annoyed me. But Miss, do you know that it's been three weeks since I was in a fight? I know you probably don't believe me, but trust me, this has never happened to me before. I hope you are not doing obeah [magic] on me."—From student who received MER therapy

The second study, conducted in 2009 by Dr. Tracey Coley, was supervised by myself and Dr. Rose Johnson,[30] another student of mine and a licensed clinical psychologist in Jamaica who also teaches at the University of the West Indies. Dr. Rose (as she's known) has used Mental and Emotional Release therapy in her private practice since 2008. Of all the tools she has learned as a therapist, Dr. Rose says that MER gives the quickest and most permanent results. "Often, a patient comes in and is so overwhelmed that they can't identify a specific issue," she explained. "When we begin by releasing their negative emotions with MER, we avoid wandering around trying to pinpoint what's going on. After that process, they are more able to focus."

So when one of her graduate students, Tracey Coley,

---

[30] Dr. Rosemarie Johnson, lecturer, Department of Sociology, Psychology, and Social Work, University of the West Indies, Mona Campus.

approached Dr. Rose about testing potential interventions for at-risk children, Dr. Rose suggested Mental and Emotional Release technique. "We know that inappropriate emotional reactions such as anger, anxiety and chronic fear are at the basis of many behavioral problems," she said. "I've used MER successfully with many children so I knew it could be effective with our at-risk children as well."

Local studies have long documented the severe challenges of many Jamaican children.[31] The government has implemented several programs to address these challenges, including improving the quality of teacher training, violence prevention programs, putting guidance counselors in schools, as well as partnering with the Jamaican business community and international funding agencies. But still, too many Jamaican children are dealing with underachievement, violence, poverty and depression, resulting in severe emotional and behavioral problems. But effective direct intervention strategies are limited, and those resulting in rapid change are nearly nonexistent.

Dr. Tracey Coley's study focused on a sample of 107 students who were enrolled in the Ministry of Education's Student Empowerment Programme, which targets students who scored 30 percent and below on the Grade Nine Achievement Test. The 107 students were specifically chosen for the study because they all exhibited serious academic, emotional, and behavioral problems. Many, if not most, of these children came from broken homes and lived in the volatile inner city. The average age of the students was fourteen years and eight months, and all were in the tenth grade at the time of the study. About 76 percent of the students in the study were boys and 24 percent girls. Via a computer program, the students were randomly divided into two groups: a test group to receive intervention with

---

[31] Crawford-Brown, 1999. Samms-Vaughn & Lambert, 1999. Evans & Johnson, 2000. Survey of Living Conditions, 2005.

MER therapy and a wait-list control group, which received intervention at the end.

In the first phase of the study, the children were assessed using standardized interviews, a behavior rating record form (focused on classroom behaviors such as punctuality, raising one's hand and waiting to be acknowledged by the teacher, listening, following directions, being prepared with books and pens, and remaining seated for the duration of class), and the Child Behavior Checklist (CBCL), a widely used and extensively validated test[32] that assesses behaviors and competencies. The CBCL includes information such as socioeconomic status and academic competence, as well as behavioral and emotions problems of the prior six months. It includes three different assessments: the Youth Self-Report Form, a Teacher Report Form, and a Parent Form.

The CBCL assesses eight syndrome measures: anxious/depressed, withdrawn/depressed, somatic complaints, social problems, thought problems, attention problems, rule-breaking behaviors, and aggressive behaviors. These syndromes can be recategorized into internalizing (i.e., anxious/depressed, withdrawn/depressed, and somatic complaints) and externalizing (i.e., rule-breaking and aggressive behavior) problems.

In this initial assessment phase, violence, disruption, aggression, defiance, and inattention were shown to be chronic in all of the students in the study. However, when students, parents, and teachers rated these problems using the CBCL, each group tended to somewhat minimize their severity. The self-ratings of students indicated that many of them considered themselves to have depression, with some physical complaints and thought problems that put them in the clinical range. Independent monitors also reported these same behaviors (e.g., aggression, defiance, inattention) and that students were often late to school, had difficulty settling down, and were often unprepared

---

[32] Achenback & Rescola, 2001.

for their classes, disruptive, aggressive, and sometimes violent. They spoke out of turn and seemed to have limited understanding of what was being taught.

After the initial assessment, the intervention phase began. Intervention for the test group involved Mental and Emotional Release therapy sessions. The children in both groups were specifically rewarded for prosocial behaviors. Each student in the test group completed three, ninety-minute sessions of the MER to release the negative emotions of anger, sadness, and fear. (Guilt and hurt were not included due to language challenges. Anger, sadness, and fear were the emotions the children clearly articulated.) At the beginning of the first session, the process of MER was explained to the student, along with the impact that anger, sadness, and fear can have on overall well-being. The benefits of releasing negative emotional baggage from the past were also discussed, and students' questions were addressed before the process started.

Initial reactions were extraordinary. Students in the test group said things like, "Miss, you fill my head with too much love. What have you left me with to deal with life? Who am I going to get bad on?" Upon releasing anger, a boy who had a history of fighting and class disruption said, "Miss, you know that sometimes people will bother you and you should just let it go. Miss, you know that I feel better. Miss, are you sure that I don't look different?" After a session, one student confessed to having been beaten by a gang years previously, a story he had never told anyone before. When asked why he told the story, he said, "I don't know, it just does not feel like it bothers me anymore."

After the intervention, parents of the students in the test group reported significantly less depression (anxious and withdrawn), rule-breaking problems, and aggressive behavior in their children when compared to parents of students in the wait-list control group. In self-assessments, students in the test group also reported significantly less depression (anxious and withdrawn), rule-breaking problems, and aggressive behaviors compared to the self-assessments of students in the control group. As one student who received MER explained it, "Miss, do you know that I haven't been in a fight with anyone since we did the things. All my friends are asking me about it. I can't afford to look soft, you know, but I am just not interested in the foolishness. I don't feel like beating up anyone."

The change in aggression level noted by the above student was observed in approximately 90 percent of the students who received MER therapy. Interestingly, teachers reported little difference in the two groups, though class monitors reported that test group students received many more rewards for good behavior in class. (Reporting by teachers may be affected by large class sizes, heavy teaching loads, and the inability of a teacher to concentrate on individual students.)

One year after the intervention, all participants in the study were contacted, but only fourteen were located: nine from the test group and five from the wait list control group. (Contact information for most of the children had changed, and it was not prudent for researchers to go to the subject's neighborhoods to inquire after them.) Five from the test group were chosen for interviews because the guidance counselors had initially identified them as having the most significant behavioral and emotional problems. The students who had received MER were all either working or attending school, while none of the students in the control group were in school or working. (In fact, one of the students from the control group was recently released from jail.)

Case Studies: Control Group with No Intervention
Statistics do not tell the tale as well as actual case studies:

Odell, who was seventeen at the time of the study, was typical of the children within the Ministry of Education's Student Empowerment Programme. He was in control group

149

and did not receive MER therapy. Odell's mother had two other children, and his father had seven altogether. He was being raised by his mother, who worked as a secretary to support him and two of his half-siblings. His teachers reported that Odell was very aggressive and often fought with other students. As he put it, "Miss, nobody wants anyone to think that they are an idiot. If these children at this school think that you are soft, it will cause lots of problems. That cannot happen to me! I have to let them know that they can't joke around with me." He had also been arrested for stealing.

A year after the study, Odell's mother told us that he had been in and out of jail even before he left school. "At first, he used to take little things, for example, he would come home with a watch and other things like that that I knew he did not have the money to buy. Then after he left school, it just got worse, and he started to rob the houses of people in the community with boys that have guns. He is in jail right now for aggravated robbery." Odell had been arrested for attempted rape of a thirteen-year-old girl.

Bevaun was another student in the control group. Also seventeen at the time of the study, Bevaun's mother had died when he was ten years old, and he lived with his grandmother. He had been suspended twice for stealing and fighting; his teachers said he was very aggressive. Bevaun did not receive MER, and he did not graduate. After high school, he continued to get into trouble in the community. A year after the study, Bevaun was interviewed and laughed as he said, "Miss, I am still giving trouble ... worse trouble. Lots of trouble like stealing, breaking into people's shops, people's houses, and I got in trouble a few months ago because I held down a thirteen-year-old girl."

Case Studies: MER Group

Results from the students who received MER therapy were dramatically different, though they began with issues and behavior problems similar to those faced by Odell and Bevaun, if not worse:

Reshay's father had died, and he was being raised by his mother and a stepfather who was physically abusive. At the time of the study, Reshay was sixteen, and his guidance counselor described him as extremely violent, moody, and reclusive. Teachers suspected that he had dyslexia, and his academic performance was very poor. During the MER process, Reshay admitted that he was researching homemade bombs and had fantasies about harming people at school.

After MER, Reshay's attitude and performance changed dramatically. He not only graduated from high school but went on to complete pre-college courses. He is currently working in a hotel restaurant and hopes to go to culinary school to become a chef. In describing his changes, Reshay told Dr. Tracey, "When I was in school it was much different. I would do things to them [students] like beat them, box them, whatever. Now I am much smarter than the average [person] toward certain things. Like I will sit down and observe more. I understand what I want and what it takes to get there. People used to say I have a bad temper. I guess it was true. But not anymore."

Ferric, a sixteen-year-old boy from a volatile inner-city community, was described as cold and hostile. He lived with his mother, who worked as an office cleaner, and his four siblings. When he was ten years old, someone pointed out Ferric's father to him. But though his father lived in the same community, Ferric had never had direct contact with him, and the man (who had fathered ten children altogether) gave the family no financial assistance.

After MER, Ferric was asked about his father. "Miss, I don't really want you to laugh at me or tell anybody this. I never met my father before. He does not have anything to do with the four of us that he had with my mother—nothing. The worst part is that he lives in the same community, maybe fifteen minutes down the lane. It used to bother me badly, but that's how it goes for all of us, so I did not want to look soft and admit that it was bothering me. I used to think about it all the time. I couldn't concentrate. Miss, that was before you and the other lady came to school and started the thing. I still think about him sometimes, but it does not bother me as much. I really don't focus on it or feel badly, like when I was at school." Ferric met requirements to graduate but left school before the ceremony to start working. He still has a full-time job and helps to support his household.

Angelina was another student who experienced significant breakthroughs with MER. The guidance counselor described this seventeen-year-old as sad, withdrawn, and inattentive in class. Her teachers said she often slept during classes. Angelina's father had disappeared, and her mother worked occasionally as a household helper. Angelina was left to care for her three younger siblings, picking them up after school, cooking for the family, and cleaning the house.

After receiving MER, Angelina proceeded to graduate from high school and create goals for her life. "Miss, I am doing hair and nails at school now, and I want to learn face. Maybe even have my own shop one day. Miss, do you know that when I was in school, I did not believe that I could do anything with my life. Me and my friends used to sit under the tree at school and talk about who would get the richest man. When you see all the girls in the community pregnant and even drop out of school, it is hard to not believe that this is going to happen to you. After graduation, I told some of my friends that I was going to school to try and do something for myself. They laughed at me, Miss. But that did not stop me from completing one year at the Human Employment and Resource Training Academy, and the lady was so impressed with me that she recommended me to a lot of people for job experience."

13

Conclusion

"It is never too late to be what you might have been."
—George Eliot

I began this book talking about the dismal statistics of mental illness we see today. On the flip side of this mental health crisis, people today more readily accept that we have control over our own thoughts and emotions, our own brains, and our own untapped potential. We now acknowledge that our thoughts and beliefs play an important part in our success or failure, our health or illness. Neuroscientists have shown us that our brains are plastic and flexible, and many of us understand that we can direct that plasticity in the directions we consciously want. We're ready to take charge, heal ourselves, and live our lives to our fullest potential.

But even though most of us know we *should* be able to change our thoughts and emotional reactions, too few people are aware of techniques that really work. Gurus who push affirmations and positive thinking as the path to fulfilling our dreams have done a disservice by not understanding or teaching the underlying concepts that can make those practices powerful.

After reading this book, you have a basic understanding of those critical underlying concepts. You may have even seen that the specific technique I've discussed here, the

Mental and Emotional Release, has the potential to improve your own life or the lives of your clients.

Let me share just a few direct quotes from clients who have experienced MER:

"I obviously wasted a lot of money on therapy over all those years. After just one [MER] session, I feel light as a feather!"

"I feel like the real me is coming out and people are responding to me differently."

"What are you doing to me?" (an email sent from a client about extraordinary changes that happened after her first MER session)

"That overwhelming grief is gone. It's now just a bittersweet feeling of nostalgia. I feel like I can move forward with my life."

"The way I see my past now is like a derelict city. I don't have to go back and fix it. Since the [MER] process, I've just moved to a different city."

"I woke up the next morning, looked in the mirror, and said to myself, 'It's lucky I have that zit on my nose. Without it, I'd be so magnificent, they wouldn't be able to handle it.' Trust me: I've never felt that way about myself before!"

"It makes me laugh. It used to be so hard to say no to people. Now it's just, 'eh.'"

Let me ask you: If you could make a significant shift for yourself, what new statement would you love to make about yourself and your life? If you work with clients, what amazing results would you like to see that you're not yet getting?

As the ancient Greek philosopher Plutarch wrote:

What we achieve inwardly will change outer reality.

So now what?

If you are interested in attending one of our trainings or finding a qualified Master Practitioner who has been certified in MER, please contact our office at (800) 800-MIND.

If you are a therapist or coach who would like to train in MER to work with your clients, please go to our website (NLP.com or EmpowermentPartnership.com) for available certification programs or my personal website (DrMatt.com) for up-to-date articles and research.

Note: In writing this, I've tried to give you a good grounding in the MER process. However, this book cannot describe everything you need to use the technique effectively. If you are interested in MER for yourself, your best bet is to call our office at (800) 800-MIND to come to one of our live trainings or work with a qualified Master Practitioner who is certified in MER. If you wish to use this technique for your clients, please view our website (DrMatt. com or EmpowermentPartnership.com) to find out about certification and available trainings.

About the Author

As an industry leader in personal development, Dr. Matt James, teaches his students how to live their most empowered life incorporating the mental, emotional, physical and spiritual aspects of Self through NLP, Ho'oponopono, Huna, Mental and Emotional Release® Therapy (MER®) and Hypnosis.

CPSIA information can be obtained
at www.ICGtesting.com
Printed in the USA
FFHW010806221218
49967979-54639FF